Tavis Smiley

How to Make
Black America Better

Tavis Smiley is a correspondent or contributor for ABC, CNN, and National Public Radio (NPR). His social and political commentary, *The Smiley Report*, is syndicated by the ABC Radio Network. Additionally, Smiley is a regular contributor to *The Tom Joyner Morning Show*, a national radio program with an audience of nine million listeners. He is the author of *Doing What's Right, Hard Left, On Air*, and *Just a Thought*, and lives in Los Angeles.

Also by Tavis Smiley

Just a Thought
Hard Left
On Air
Doing What's Right

How to Make Black America Better

How to Make Black America Better

Leading African Americans Speak Out

Tavis Smiley

Anchor Books
A Division of Random House, Inc.
New York

FIRST ANCHOR BOOKS EDITION, JANUARY 2002

Copyright © 2001 by Tavis Smiley

All rights reserved under International and Pan-American Copyright
Conventions. Published in the United States by Anchor Books, a division of
Random House, Inc., New York, and simultaneously in Canada by Random
House of Canada Limited, Toronto. Originally published in hardcover in the
United States by Doubleday, a division of Random House, Inc.,
New York, in 2001.

Anchor Books and colophon are registered trademarks of
Random House, Inc.

The Library of Congress has cataloged the Doubleday edition as follows:
Smiley, Tavis, 1964–
How to make Black America better : leading African Americans speak out /
Tavis Smiley.—1st ed.
p. cm.
ISBN 0-385-50214-1 (alk. paper)
1. African Americans—Social conditions—1975– —Quotations, maxims, etc.
2. African Americans—Civil rights—Quotations, maxims, etc. 3. African
Americans—Race identity—Quotations, maxims, etc. 4. Social values—
United States—Quotations, maxims, etc. 5. Conduct of life—Quotations,
maxims, etc. 6. African Americans—Quotations. I. Title.
E185.86 .S633 2001
305.896'073—dc21 00-065610
CIP

Anchor ISBN: 0-385-72087-4

Book design by Chris Welch

w w w . a n c h o r b o o k s . c o m

Printed in the United States of America
10 9 8 7 6 5 4 3

For
the students
of the
Tavis Smiley Foundation's
Youth to Leaders
Empowering today's youth for tomorrow

Acknowledgments

I'm pressing on the upward way,
New heights I'm gaining every day.

Still praying as I'm onward bound,
Lord, plant my feet on higher ground.

My heart has no desire to stay,
Where doubts arise and fears dismay.

Though some may dwell where these abound,
My prayer, my aim is higher ground.

Anyone who has ever seen me on the lecture circuit has no doubt heard me recite these words to one of my favorite Black spirituals, *Higher Ground*.

For me, life is about taking full advantage of His new mercies every day and finding a way to reach that higher ground.

I am fortunate to have a wonderful and intimate group of people hoisting me up every day as I attempt to do my small part to help make Black America better.

First, to my immediate family: my mother, Joyce Marie Smiley; my father, Emory G. Smiley; and my nine siblings: Pamela, Phyllis, Garnie, Paul, Patrick, Maury, Derwin, Weldon, and Dion.

To the folks who I love just like family who put up with me every day in our work at The Smiley Group, Inc.: Wendi Chavis, Kathye Davenport, Andrea Foggy-Paxton, Dawn Fong, Shari Randolph, Raymond Ross, and Karla Thierry.

Special thanks to Sonya Ross, Stephanie Land, Noreen McClendon, Ken Browning, and Errol Collier. Without these folks, especially Sonya, this book would still be in my head and not on paper.

To the world's best editor, Roger Scholl, thank you seems so shallow, but thank you.

For Chi Blackburn and Aubrey O. Prince, thanks for just sticking around here.

To my pastor, Bishop Noel Jones, and my dearest Iyanla Vanzant, thanks for all the coaching, counseling, and caretaking. It's all right now.

Finally, to Harold W. Patrick and Denise Pines. Can't imagine two people who I'd rather share a foxhole with . . . but not for too many days! Thanks for your abiding friendship, sage counsel, and unwavering support.

Contents

Part I:

Part II:

Part III:

Introduction

Tavis Smiley

A s African Americans, each of us must bear the burden of try-ing to save the soul of Black America.

I say *burden* because, let's face it, there is much work to be done and the challenges which now face our folks are daunting and complex. Worse, we have not yet been able to convince every brother and sister to share in the burden by shouldering his or her own load. The fact is, we don't have a single African American to waste.

Many of those who best understand our struggle, because they were there on the front lines fighting the good fight and keeping the faith, have passed on. Thurgood Marshall. Daisy Bates. Leon Higginbotham. Other Black national treasures like Rosa Parks, John Hope Franklin, and Dorothy Height are yet with us, but have more days behind them than in front of them.

These brave leaders and countless others have paved the way for the first generation of young Black leaders not born of struggle; the first generation of Black leaders who cannot compare the "before" and "after" pictures, because we were born in the post–civil rights era. We represent the fruits of their labor and the hopes of their dreams. Yet too many of us are abrogating our responsibility to our ancestors and to each other. They lived for a cause; we live, too often, just because.

We seem to have forgotten the words of Benjamin E. Mays, who said, "He who starts behind in the great race of life must forever remain behind, or run faster than the man in front."

It's time for us to pick up the pace.

I love the wise old saying about the gazelle and the lion. When the gazelle wakes up in the morning, he knows there's somebody out there to eat him. So he'd better be up running. And the lion? When the lion wakes up, he knows that if he doesn't catch anything he'll starve. The point is, it doesn't matter if you're a gazelle or a lion, you'd better wake up in the morning running.

That's how every Black person in America should approach life, as well.

Whether we're young or old, rich and famous, or struggling and trying to come up, every morning we have to wake up running, doing everything we can to help make Black America better.

Recently, I sat down to lunch with John H. Johnson, the visionary founder and publisher of *Ebony* and *Jet* magazines. I have long admired Mr. Johnson for his personal contribution and his mission to chronicle the efforts of ordinary and extraordinary Black folks who have done their part to help make Black America better. As I sat there in his private dining room atop the Johnson Publishing Company's Chicago headquarters overlooking Lake Michigan, it struck me that with all Mr. Johnson had accomplished personally and professionally, despite his advanced age and the fact that he clearly was not in the best of health, he was continuing his lifelong mission to help make Black America better. He did that in part by sharing with me the wisdom that only a Black man who has succeeded against all the odds can know.

What I hope to share with you in this book are a few of the simple steps each of us can take to make a meaningful contribution to our community and our country. I had enough good sense to know that when it came to articulating an agenda to improve Black America, I needed a chorus of voices. No one person stands as the spokesperson for Black America.

And so I reached out to a number of Black America's most accomplished and prominent individuals, from various fields of endeavor, to ask them their thoughts on how we can make Black America better. I was fascinated with the thoughts and ideas they expressed, and I think you will be as well.

How to Make Black America Better is further enriched by excerpts from the exciting discussion and opinions voiced at a historic symposium I hosted in Los Angeles before the Democratic National Convention entitled *Advocacy in the Next Millennium: New Paradigms for Progress.* The forum featured a dazzling array of Black America's best and brightest opinion-makers and thought-leaders, and I think you'll find what they had to say both compelling and provocative.

As I grow older, I'm becoming more and more convinced that we make life a lot more complicated than it really is. Sure, we all have our ups and downs. And, yes, we face unique challenges as African Americans. But while our problems may be daunting, they need not be devastating. In fact, I would argue whether all of our problems are really problems. If a solution to your problem exists, then you really don't have a problem! A *real* problem begs for a solution.

We are an overcoming people. Always have been. Always will be.

A reporter asked me recently a rather interesting question. He wanted to know what I thought was missing in the contemporary Black struggle.

My answer was simple. What's missing in our struggle, I told him, is a sense of urgency. Don't ask me why, but Black folks have a high threshold for pain. Well, it's time to stop enduring the pain and take active steps to overcome it. One of these mornings we have to wake up running.

Dr. Martin Luther King, Jr., was fond of saying that "The time is always ripe to do right."

We have some unfinished business to attend to in the beloved community. My hope—and the hope of so many of my esteemed contributors—is that after reading *How to Make Black America Better*, you will not return to Black business as usual. But rather you will take up the task of making Black America well, with a renewed sense of purpose and urgency.

Enough already. Let's crack the pages and get to work!

And, as always, remember Big Momma's words:

> *Once a task you've first begun,*
> *Never finish until it's done.*
> *Be the labor great or small,*
> *Do it well or not at all.*

Part

I

Ten Challenges to Black America

In America, there seems to be a top 10 list for everything these days. I didn't set out with the goal of writing a top 10 list about Black America. In fact, I thought hard about how to adjust my list to avoid a "top 10" stigma. But this was the number the list naturally organized itself into, and I realized in the end that the length of the list is not as important as the depth of what is on it.

While the list in no way covers everything that we can or should do to make Black America better, it does provide a starting point, a point of departure. I created it to be a meaningful but manageable list that our people can get their arms around.

The list is organized in no particular order of importance. But I do start with challenging every Black American to think Black first, simply because any effort to make Black America better must start with a conscious effort to do *something*. We need a mind-set that makes it clear that we control our own destiny, and that through discernment, diligence, and dignity we can overcome *today*, not someday.

There is nothing we have done (or left undone) as part of the Black American experience that we cannot recover from or build upon. But as with problems of a medical nature, there must be a diagnosis, a prognosis, and a treatment before we can look to a cure. We already know what's wrong, we already know how to fix it. The question is: Do we have the courage to take the medicine that will help make Black America better? So, while these challenges and this book are not a panacea, my hope is that they can serve as a starting point.

Think Black First, 100 Percent of the Time

Whenever we engage in business deals, whenever we have work for hire or contracts to be shared, or even if we're doing something as mundane as shopping, we should tell ourselves:

"I must find someone Black for this job. I must find someplace Black to spend this money." After all, we cannot blame the white man for our problems if we don't try to solve them ourselves. Our mission should be, first and foremost, to uplift the race.

How many times, in the past year alone, can you recall hearing another Black person rail about how we give our dollars to every community but our own? Thinking Black requires more than altering our behavior as consumers or deciding to settle down in Black neighborhoods. It requires us to really part with some ingrained economic habits. We have fine examples in pop culture. Rather than watch top fashion designers, such as Ralph Lauren and Tommy Hilfiger, corner the market by appropriating hip-hop styles, Sean "Puffy" Combs and Russell Simmons countered with clothing lines of their own: Sean John and Phat Farm. The same holds true for the line of FUBU gear. FUBU's name stands for "for us, by us." And young Black Americans have responded by making FUBU one of the country's largest-selling design labels. Walter Latham, noticing a paucity of venues for Black comedy, brought together four Black comedians, dubbed them "The Kings of Comedy," and put them out on a national tour that was wildly successful. When Latham was ready to do a movie about the tour, he went with a Black director, Spike Lee.

Thinking Black first is an easy commitment to make. But don't be fooled; it is not the easiest commitment to keep. Thinking Black 100 percent of the time, however, doesn't mean we're required to act on our intentions all the time. In fact, getting our intentions translated into action can be a real challenge: At times, a Black alternative may not be available. And many of us have horror stories of being left in a lurch by a fellow Black person who simply failed to deliver. Just prior to the start of the 2000 Democratic National Convention in Los Angeles, for example, I sought out Black videographers to tape the symposium on advocacy I hosted (excerpts of which appear in this book). I hired three who came with good recommendations. To my dismay, they produced footage that was of poor quality and not at all worth the cost. We all have to realize that thinking Black is a two-way street. Our businesses can no longer limp along in the new millennium on the excuse that Black customers will support them. When we, as Black consumers, spend our money, we deserve quality, because by virtue of being Black we had to work *harder* to get our money. In my experience, this type of problem has been the exception rather than the rule. Just one experience like that can have a chilling effect, however, on the Black consumer; it can make us reluctant to choose Black the next time and leave us braced for substandard treatment when we do. I recognize that there are times when I can't do business with a

Black person. But I always think Black first and always try to keep my business in the community.

For some areas in our lives, thinking Black is automatic. When we want soul food, a good barber or beauty shop, or place to worship, we know where to go. Plenty of Black people take our cars to a Black mechanic, regardless of whether he has his own shop or is replacing parts beneath a shade tree in his Backyard. But more often than not, we don't take thinking Black to the next level. We don't put diligence into supporting Black stockbrokers, lawyers, agents, doctors, dentists, Web sites. We have ourselves convinced that in those arenas, the white man's ice is colder. We complain all the time about the difficulties of being Black, of being dissed, of being misunderstood in our day-to-day dealings. Yet we have to be challenged all the time to give such business to a fellow Black person. There are other areas where we just flat out give our business away without even asking whether we could have found a Black person to support it, such as furniture design. C'mon, people! *All* of us! I shouldn't even have to say this in this book. Start by at least considering the Black possibilities. It offers one of the few sure ways for Black America to climb on out of the abyss. If we can't help ourselves and look out for each other, how can we expect anyone else to?

Look Past What Whites Are Doing to Us to See What We Are Doing to Ourselves

A lot of our actions as Black people have been directed at trying to get white people to change. There are too many of us who allow our life decisions to be governed by the "statement" we feel our actions might make to white people. The perceptions of white people even find their way into decisions we make about the clothes we buy or the hairstyles we wear. During the civil rights movement, we devoted a good bit of our energy and time to making it clear that we are equal, that our aspirations, concerns, and feelings about life are the same as those of white people, in the hope that the white community would come to understand and accept us as equals. Today, we can no longer afford to do this. It is time to give up on the idea of changing white people and seek change from within, among ourselves. For in the final analysis, it's not about their misbehavior but our behavior. Rather than analyze whether it is easier to attract bees with honey or vinegar, we should ask ourselves why we feel compelled to attract the bees in the first place.

As our society becomes more multiracial and multiethnic, our numbers and the power of our combined voices speak for themselves. It is becoming more in vogue to be a person of color. White Americans are being confronted with the need to change their views and perceptions, and already we see signs of resistance, the desperate attempt to change the rules to put off this sea change: rollbacks in affirmative action programs; tightened restrictions on immigration; a push for vouchers to finance private schooling at the expense of public education. There are so many issues where the rules are in flux because of a growing realization among white people that they are becoming a minority and may no longer be able to control the game. So they're trying to change the rules, instead. So why look to white America for recognition or acceptance? As Black Americans, we need to focus on our "selfs": self-determination, self-reliance, and self-respect.

I'm less certain that we are as self-determining a people as we once were. And by self-determination I mean our determination to control what we create and who we are. In the previous challenge, I praised the impresarios of hip-hop culture for thinking Black first. However, I do not understand, for the life of me, how such a purely Black creation as hip-hop slid out of our control. Much like its predecessor—jazz—hip-hop is an astounding pop culture phenomenon in modern America. We are the writers, the producers, the singers and rappers, the fashion designers, the filmmakers in control of the imagery. But too few of us are the *moguls* in control of the dollars. Indeed, we can count the number of hip-hop moguls on our fingers. If Berry Gordy could create Motown—and retain single-handed control over "the Motown sound"—forty years ago, don't tell me we lack the capacity to create and control hip-hop now. There are many Black artists with a record deal or their own label as a subsidiary of a larger label. But too few of them have taken up the reins of their art like Master P, founder of No Limit Records.

A lack of self-determination, in turn, thwarts our ability to be self-reliant. Black people are a proud people. I would argue that no other race has worked harder to build this country. Yet somehow, we have managed to become the abiding symbol of the welfare state. No matter how many times Jesse Jackson, Sr., points out that there are more white than Black people on welfare, the politicians *we* elect turn right around and level an argument that the Black community does not believe in personal responsibility. Why? Because some of us have allowed the fact that this country owes a debt to us, the children of the slaves who built it, to become an excuse for avoiding self-reliance. We are preoccupied with the notion that someone "owes" us something. As a result, we devote more energy to sitting around waiting for the payoff than getting up and getting our own.

I see attitude manifested most clearly in our behavior toward our own families. Far too many Black Americans in the post–World War II generations see our parents as tickets to a rent-free, responsibility-free existence. We barely pause to think about the daily burdens this creates for them, much less the fact that it robs them of the retirement for which they worked all their lives. In my own family of nine siblings, not once have I or my two sisters returned home to live with our mother. No matter how much we have had to struggle, we remained independent. But all seven of my brothers have run home occasionally as life has thrown them a curve. I want to discuss family relations more in a later chapter. The point here is that this sort of behavior has a devastating impact on our overall self-reliance and self-worth.

While America does owe us something, we owe each other far more. Martin Luther King, Jr., once said the check that the United States wrote to its Black citizens has come back marked INSUFFICIENT FUNDS. But let's suppose America suddenly decided to make good on that bounced check. How could we deposit it? Our Black American account is either consistently over-drawn or closed altogether. As long as we run a deficit with each other, we cannot in good conscience expect America to pay its debt to us. Clearing this deficit begins with self-reliance.

We should approach our collective self-respect much like an emergency on an airplane. In the event of a sudden loss of cabin pressure, we should put the oxygen mask on ourselves first before assisting others. In other words, an individual brother or sister cannot help fellow Black Americans survive if they themselves are dying. Only if we are healthy individuals will we have the energy and strength to help our communities. A lack of self-respect is, in many ways, emotionally crippling us. Because so many of us don't respect ourselves, we feel free to abridge the rights of other people in our communities. In explaining why so many young Black men kill each other, author Nathan McCall once suggested that, for these individuals, killing another Black person is actually a form of suicide. After all, a young brother who doesn't care to live himself certainly doesn't care whether his peers live or die. In the constant game of survival that is so much a part of being Black in America, self-preservation is the order of the day. There's no room to thrive when you're trying to survive. Survival is a basic instinct; you will do anything to endure. When you're playing the survival game, self-respect is sacrificed at worst and becomes secondary at best. Once we practice self-determination, self-reliance, and self-respect, it really doesn't matter, then, what white people do or what they think of us.

Every Black American Should Put Family First

L ike charity, self-reliance begins at home. If life is like base-ball, then our families are the farm teams that prepare us to play in the big leagues,

During the 1980s and 1990s, many of us began serving as mentors to troubled Black youth. It was an admirable act of altruism. But how many of us spent Saturdays at the community center helping someone else's child with homework or treating them to a movie, without considering whether our own siblings, nieces, nephews, or cousins needed similar attention from us? Even in matters of philanthropy, we tend to look past our own families. It is time for us to realize that when we feel the need to shape the life of a child, we can often start by looking no further than our own families.

There was a time in the Black community when family always came first. With all the pressures that slavery put on us, family had to come first. In *Roots,* we saw Alex Haley's family fighting over several centuries to stay together, even as relatives were sold, chased off, or taken away by war. Between slavery and the days of Jim Crow segregation, has there ever been such a thing as a traditional nuclear family for us? When some of us ran off from our children, more often than not it was our families who took those children in. We even took in those who became part of our families in our hearts, who were not part of our bloodline. The extended family has always been part of our reality.

But nowadays, there is a "me first" mentality among us that is powerfully destructive. Part of this is the result of the American condition. The family as an institution in America is under a tremendous strain, given the rates of divorce and domestic violence. The fact is, Black America tends to suffer from such pressures to a greater degree than overall society, and so this is an even greater problem for us. An increasing number of young mothers and fathers seem unwilling to put their children's needs ahead of their own desires.

Putting family first is simple. It means respecting our mothers and doing whatever we can to ease their burdens. It means shedding hostility toward absent fathers. It means *being* fathers to our children. It means putting a priority on creating an environment in which our children can flourish. It means actively establishing our families, rather than reacting to an unplanned family. It means putting an end to the feud that caused someone to stop speaking to their sisters and brothers or made them mad at their aunt, uncle, or cousin. It means giving our families a spiritual base. And it requires us to think legacy, not lineage, when it comes to our families. We are not all born rich and lucky. However, we all have the capacity and, more importantly, the responsibility to nurture families that are healthy, secure, and poised to prosper. We have to care less about complexion and grade of hair and care more about what we put in the hearts and minds of the children we create. There are some things that government can do to help the disenfranchised among us put family first. The government can and should provide assistance with child care, paid family leave, tax credits, preschool education, and gun safety restrictions, if it means our families will be made that much more whole. But as we saw with welfare reform, government will always draw a line. And that's where we as individuals need to step into the breach. We already are taking steps in that direction, as we witnessed with the pledge of atonement our brothers took at 1995's Million Man March and the similar pledge our sisters took in the Million Woman March that followed. These bonds were solidified in 2000 with the Million Family March.

Remember, our family is our legacy. No matter what decisions you make within your life, they are bound to have the greatest impact on those you love and who love you the most: your family.

Black Americans Must Consider the Consequences of Their Actions

There is an old adage that goes: "When and where I enter, the whole race enters with me." To put it in more contemporary terms, as long as you're Black, you have to represent. Any time an African American is given an opportunity to showcase his or her abilities, it offers one more opportunity to make or break the chances for African Americans who attempt to come through the door behind you. There simply are no days when we can wipe the color off our skins and just be ourselves. It may not be fair and/or make us feel good, but that's the reality. It's the price we pay for being Black.

When Latrell Sprewell choked his coach, he did not deny a other brother a chance to play in the National Basketball Association. However, he did refuel in the minds of many people the false belief that Black men are naturally violent. Now millions of brothers who are not as wealthy or famous as Sprewell must live down the bad name that Spree earned for them. Neither Sprewell nor Allen Iverson, who sparked a national controversy over the lyrics to a song he included on his new rap CD, considered the consequences of their actions. Iverson challenged people who were man enough to carry a gun to pull the trigger. But there is a difference in the two cases.

I'm not sure Latrell ever really got it. Iverson, on the other hand, recognized his mistake when he was confronted with it and both apologized and agreed to pull the lines out of the song. Every brother who has committed a crime—especially crimes against white victims—has, in those victims' eyes, helped to criminalize an entire race of people. Yes, there is discrimination in law enforcement, as we have known for years. And that is why the fact that there is even one Black criminal out there makes it that much harder for us to shed the stigma of being seen as criminals.

Of course, such stigma is not limited to matters of crime and punishment. When a Black executive engages in suspect business practices, he runs the risk in our society of tainting other Black executives who are honest. Hollywood entertainers who accept demeaning roles diminish the opportunities for others to land meaningful roles. Although John Singleton's visionary 1991 film, *Boyz N the Hood,* won critical acclaim, the rash of cheap, cloned so-called "hood movies" that it spawned made it difficult for legitimate scripts with socially redemptive messages to even get studio consideration. Could those cheap clones have been made had Black actors refused those roles? While the reputations of individual actors who accept such stereotypical roles may not be hurt, scores of others behind them—writers, actors, and directors—*are.*

We all need to consider the consequences of our actions. I include here our Black stars. They have to accept the challenge to continually present a positive image, because even the slightest negativity can be devastating. Lil' Kim can't be hoochie *and* Gucci! At some point, she must consider the consequences to the lyrics of her songs. At some point, Lil' Kim must realize how many young girls are clocking what she wears in public and now think it is okay to be scantily clad in any setting. What we do in public matters.

As Molière said, "It is not only what we do, but also what we do not do for which we are accountable." We too must bear responsibility for the consequences of our inaction. When we don't stand up for the causes in which we believe, we must share the blame when things go awry. When we don't show up for PTA meetings or parent-teacher conferences, we are responsible too when our children fail. When we don't fulfill our obligation to talk to our children about sex, we are responsible too when they fall victim to unplanned pregnancies or sexually transmitted diseases. When some of us don't pay bills, it makes other African Americans look suspect to mortgage lenders and credit card companies. Marion Barry's failings while mayor of the District of Columbia made the Black voters who put him in office yet again seem, to the rest of the country, as if they were not very bright or politically astute. And by failing to think in the long term, Black voters of the District incurred the wrath of Congress, which promptly stripped the city of self-rule and installed a control board to oversee the elected officials' decisions.

This is not another debate over whether Charles Barkley was right when he said he was not a role model. I'm not suggesting that people have to be role models. The point here is that each of us, as African Americans, has to buy into the notion of being a race model. The term "role model" implies having met a certain standard of perfection voluntarily. A "race model" has no choice *but* to meet that standard. The role model plays to a visible audience of people who choose to admire him. The race model plays to an invisible audience he doesn't even know is admiring him. A role model doesn't bear the burden of having to be all things to all people. A race model does. So let's set out with the goal of being the best Black people we can be. The race is bound to rise as a result.

Every Black American Should See Him- or Herself as Part of a Larger Black Community

The struggles that African Americans face are not markedly different from those faced by people of African descent around the world. In fact, one thing you see when you travel outside the United States is that our struggles and theirs are inextricably linked. If you go to Cuba, you'll quickly realize that Afro-Cubanos sit on the bottom rung of the economic ladder there in much the same way that we do in America. If you go to South Africa, you'll see that while apartheid no longer exists and the Black majority wields more political clout than ever before, the vestiges of apartheid still are cutting Black South Africans off from society's mainstream, just as segregation caused Black Americans to get left behind. In Britain, Blacks are struggling to win seats in Parliament, just as we are fighting to gain a greater presence in Congress. In a perfect world, these shared struggles would be the foundation for a strong bond between us and the rest of the Black world. But the fact is, we in America tune out the rest of the world. There are parallels between the Hutu-Tutsi tribal conflict that fed the 1994 genocide in Rwanda and our own experiences with Black-on-Black crime. Yet we, as a race, remain disconnected from the situation in Rwanda, even as thousands of hacked, mutilated bodies turned up in the rivers.

Why are we today so silent about the potential for more Hutu-Tutsi genocidal violence in Burundi? If we can understand and have pride in Nelson Mandela's journey from political prisoner to president, why do we remain so disconnected from South Africa's struggles to battle the AIDS epidemic? Fifteen years ago, our protests and calls for disinvestment were the catalyst that brought down apartheid and set Mandela's release in motion. But why are we so content, fifteen years later, to rest on our laurels and believe things in South Africa are progressing nicely? I understand that Africa's problems are so complex that they can leave us feeling paralyzed and powerless to do anything about them. But, people, we barely inject our voices into the policy decisions that our government makes about Africa or any other continent or country. It's not as if we don't know that U.S. foreign policy has enormous ramifications for the entire African diaspora. We wouldn't be so dismissive, I believe, if we better grasped our standing in the global Black community.

We can begin to enhance the Black world community by expanding our myopic view of world issues. We rarely have conversations about foreign policy in our communities. Holding such conversations would result in a clarion call from us for our government to step up its peacekeeping commitments in Liberia and Sierra Leone. We should insist that our government do all it can to fix African problems, considering the role the United States played in propping up African dictators for the sake of Cold War strategy. Instead, we sit numbly in front of our television sets, watching tragedy after tragedy rake the African continent, saying "Ain't that a shame" without realizing our tax dollars made most of these things happen.

When our brothers and sisters throughout the world are harmed, we too are harmed. We are being disrespected at home for not lending our voices to foreign policy decisions made abroad, and Africans worldwide are being disrespected abroad because we're being disrespected at home. This is also a strategic failure, in the sense that African Americans are a vanishing breed, and we're not trying to bolster our numbers with Africans, who are clearly our brothers and sisters. For white people, assimilation of immigrants from European countries bolsters their numbers. Why are we not reaching out to Africans?

Every Black person benefits when we, the Black people in the most powerful country in the world, speak out. Look at yourself. Chances are, if we're disconnected on a global scale, we're not paying attention to our own people, either. Those of us who understand our problems locally usually have an awareness of Black people on an international level.

We can only gain a broader world view through greater understanding, and gaining understanding begins with following the news, reading about life and politics in other countries, and taking the time to talk to Blacks from other countries that we come into contact with. It means, if possible, traveling beyond the United States borders. Many of us don't even have passports— we consider international travel to be the domain of the rich and famous. We must let that mentality go. If you are too strapped for cash to afford a trip abroad, then try to seek out people from other countries—teachers, students, businessmen—when they arrive on our shores. For example, every Black college has African students, yet many of us do not even try to get to know them. Sometimes establishing a link can be as simple as striking up a conversation with a cabdriver. The bottom line is we've got to gain a better understanding of the African diaspora and the world around us. We will be politically, socially, economically bankrupt if we don't.

Every Black American Must Preserve His or Her Health— Physically, Emotionally, Psychologically, and Spiritually

It is astounding that with all of the talk, all of the statistics, charts, and reports on the deteriorating health of Black America, we are not more serious about taking care of ourselves. We all know the old truism if you don't have your health you don't have anything, and yet in nearly every category of illness, we are at or near the top of the list. We're not eating right, we're not getting enough exercise, we're not taking our vitamins, we're not doing the basics. Now, I'm no Mr. Universe. Like many of us, I struggle to maintain my weight and live a healthy lifestyle. I get constant reminders from my audience to take care of myself. Because Black folks will tell you when you're looking tired!

Brothers and sisters, we can no longer run from our health issues. Our very survival is at stake. Every day we ignore a symptom or two, we put off visits to the doctor, and inevitably we perish from treatable diseases. Every day we see disproportionate numbers of Black people on the street, homeless and sick, and we just dismiss them. Then there are countless numbers we don't see, living on the margins of our communities as they struggle with mental illness or addiction, and we don't acknowledge them. Even in our families, we just say, "Oh, that nigga's crazy." We just lock 'em in a rear bedroom. We as a people are struggling under the weight of a lot of social ills and pressure, conditions that depress us. When depression is properly treated, those who suffer from it can lead normal lives. But in our communities, depression tends to go untreated, and too often untreated depression manifests through other social ills: homelessness, domestic violence, child abandonment, drug use, alcohol abuse. We tell ourselves that we don't have the financial resources to deal with these problems—but that really is just a crutch.

Even when our depression is not of a clinical nature, we as Black Americans are carrying around a lot of emotional hurt. Women *and* men. We're carrying pain about our childhoods, about our parents, our brothers and sisters, our relationships. We use one another, we abuse one another, some of us never get over one another. We harbor anger—lifetime anger—toward past loves for a litany of unmet expectations. And too many of us refuse to talk to anyone about these problems, much less see a therapist.

I, for one, never fully appreciated my mother's wit and wisdom—until I was really, really hurt by a woman. For six months, the pain of my breakup with this woman was eating me up inside. I was emotionally wrecked and trying to go on in my professional capacity as if nothing had happened. Typically, I would end the day in a hotel room in some strange city, crying through my pain. But once I sat down and began having heart-to-heart talks with my mother about it, my pain started to subside. Sometimes easing our pain is as simple as talking to someone about it.

Many of us wallow in the "brothers are dogs, sisters are trifling" rhetoric, and then we start to *believe* it. We cannot afford to lug this emotional baggage.

What keeps all of our health issues in balance is a solid spiritual relationship. We have to be secure in the belief that there is a higher power and a higher purpose for our existence. I believe that as long as you have faith in a higher power, you can't go crazy. There is an old spiritual that says if you take one step, God'll take two. I believe we're bound to be held in good stead if we maintain our connection to a higher power. That connection got us through slavery and out of slavery—it is definitely strong enough to get us through this new millennium.

If you don't have your health, you won't be around for the struggle. We need every soldier we can get; we don't have a single Black body to lose. So, please, take care of yours.

Every Black American Should Develop an Economic Plan

America is enjoying a period of unprecedented economic prosperity. As Black Americans, we'll be out of line if we do not develop an economic plan to gain a share of that prosperity. Without an economic plan, we will not have the means to recycle Black dollars, maintain a decent quality of life, or maintain an economic future beyond the next paycheck.

Many of us are filled with a desire to give back to our communities. Others of us *are* giving back, but in the least tax-deductible kinds of ways. And that's where the problems come in. We provide our families with infusions of cash, we help with paying bills, we make loans that often are not repaid, we support the business enterprises of our friends more out of loyalty than fiscal sensibility. Sometimes those obligations drain us so much that we can't even begin to think about giving money to the standard types of charitable contributions. While it may seem cruel to curb some of the above-mentioned activities, we need to do so if we're going to truly invest in our communities.

Outside of that, we must save for ourselves for a rainy day. We must stop living beyond our means. C'mon. Do we all need to drive a Mercedes-Benz or a BMW when a good Ford or Honda will do? Too many of us spend money we don't have on things we don't need, in order to impress people we don't even like. A little plastic surgery—as in cutting up those credit cards—wouldn't hurt. We must abandon our fear of investment and diversify the items we do invest in. We can't keep pouring our resources into real estate while shying away from the stock market. If you're scared of the stocks, start with what you know. If you eat at McDonald's or wear Nike shoes, explore investing in Nike or McDonald's stock. Or put your money in a mutual fund or an index fund. Get a financial adviser if you need one. You don't have to be wealthy to afford a little professional help.

Once we get our personal finances in order, we will be better positioned to help our communities. In its July 2000 issue, *Black Enterprise* magazine offered some concrete suggestions for giving Black, and they deserve to be highlighted here. Please read and heed:

- Make charitable contributions to nonprofit organizations that you can relate to.
- Give to your church.
- Give in-kind gifts, such as clothing, furniture, or office equipment.
- Volunteer your time.
- Identify a volunteer project your family can do together.
- Sponsor community activities, such as conferences, seminars, or holiday toy drives.
- Serve as a mentor.
- Sit on the board of advisers for a community group or nonprofit organization.
- Invest in socially responsible mutual funds.
- Establish a trust as part of your estate plan.

Make Education the Number-One Priority for Every Black American

Malcolm X said an education is our passport to the future, for tomorrow belongs to those who prepare for it today. But the sad truth is too many of us push the pursuit of knowledge to the bottom of our list of priorities. We ignore the examples of history—from the slaves who learned to read, even though they were forbidden to do so, to the scores of Black Americans who endured beatings and death threats in the fight to integrate public schools—and we allow our children's minds, the most precious commodity we have, to suffer. Too often, we don't show up at PTA meetings, school board meetings, or parent-teacher conferences—that is, until our children become a discipline problem. Even then, teachers and principals have to track some of us down and beg us to come in to talk about it, and some of us show up cussin' and kickin', mad at the people who are doing their level best to educate our children against considerable odds! Is it any wonder that our children don't believe school is important? How often do our children actually see us in the pursuit of knowledge? How many of us actually read to our children? Take them to a bookstore or the public library? While we sit around articulating lofty goals about reading, libraries in many of our communities are being closed down or are cutting back on their hours. Would this be happening if education were our number-one priority?

We can truly begin making education our number-one priority with simple actions: reading to our children, taking the time to help them with their homework. Some of us shy away from these activities because we're busy, because we haven't been in school for a long time, or because we may not have been good at these things ourselves. But our children discover what is important to us by the amount of time they see us investing in those things. They know watching football is important to Daddy when they see him doing that all day on Sunday. They will know that school and homework and reading and knowledge are important if they see Mommy and Daddy encouraging them to do it.

We need to make education our number-one priority because right now, there are more changes afoot than ever before. We're losing the fight to save public education. We are seeing states aggressively pursue using public dollars to fund private education. The numbers of Black college graduates choosing education as a career are dwindling. One by one, states are wiping out the affirmative action programs through which many young Black people went to college. Which means once we do get our children graduated from beleaguered public school systems, access to higher education will be increasingly difficult for many of them. Yet at home, we're not taking the steps *we* can take to bolster what our children are learning in class. We'll buy our children a Sega Genesis PlayStation, but we won't buy encyclopedias! We can't keep blaming the system for failing our kids when we are failing our kids, too. Too many of our children get labeled as uneducable.

Because of crime and discipline problems, more school systems are instituting so-called "zero tolerance" policies, through

which disproportionate numbers of our children are being ex-
pelled. Kids are kids and prone to make mistakes. There ought to
be very few things a child can do for which there is *zero* tolerance. As a matter of fact, if anyone should have zero tolerance,
it's our children! Zero tolerance for dilapidated facilities, for
poorly trained teachers, for ineffective administrators. But none
of that will change if we don't move education to the top of our
lists.

Encourage the Black Church to Do More

The real work of the church does not take place on Sunday. It happens Monday through Saturday. The real work of the church is not about singing, shouting, or raising an offering, it is about effecting change in our communities. The Black church has long held our communities together. It has fed us, clothed us, nurtured us, sheltered us from social storms, harbored us in times of trouble. So why are so many of our houses of worship moving away from this historical role? I am troubled to see that many churches have a singles ministry, but lack programs to care for senior citizens, comfort those recovering from addictions, or feed the homeless. Yes, many of our churches are still providing dinner after services—but now they are selling it. Sometimes the steeple has a leak in it, and the pastor is driving a Lexus.

The Black church is one of the last bastions of gender apartheid. Black women are the backbones of the church, but somehow they are not considered qualified to preach and minister. The African Methodist Episcopal Church has been with us for 200 years, yet didn't name its first female bishop, the Rev. Vashti Murphy McKenzie, until last year (2000).

It is time for the Black church to create a new paradigm, to build a new construct. Too many shy away from preaching a message of social responsibility. Nowhere is this more evident than in the Black church's ringing silence about the spread of AIDS in the Black community. The overriding concern we hear is that AIDS is the result of sin. Where is the compassion for the afflicted?

We are seeing Black churches grow larger and larger, evolving into suburban "megachurches" with thousands of members and their own television programs. The problem is, these mega-churches are being built farther away from where Black people live. It seems as if even the churches are trying to escape the inner cities. Yet that's precisely where they need to be! Moreover, the people who are in church every Sunday sometimes are there for the wrong reasons. They're filling the pews because they heard that a particular church is the *in* place to be, because the minister is developing a national following, or because the choir has won critical acclaim. Again, where is the sense of a higher calling?

During the height of the civil rights movement, the Black church was the prophetic witness. In the 1960s, Jesse Jackson, Sr., was one of many such ministers and leaders. Today, he is almost a singular breed, a minister who is challenging the nation to live up to its social responsibilities. The Black church has always been the vanguard of our struggle. It cannot afford to become invisible. We have to make it accountable to the people. The first step toward challenging the Black church to do better is for us to GO to church. JOIN in. If we want it to change, we have to place ourselves on the front lines to help make that change happen. After all, the Black church can't improve if there are no people in it.

Every Black American Should Establish a Black American Legacy

Too many of us are indifferent to what's going on around us. We tune the world around us out. Because we spend so much time struggling with the small picture, we don't look at the big picture. We don't take the time to consider how people are going to remember us. We don't think about doing the best we can with what we've been given or about leaving behind a legacy of commitment and progress.

The word "legacy" may sound daunting. And it's true, establishing a legacy is no easy task. Building a legacy means you have to figure out where you stand on matters that require courage, persistence, faith, principle, vision. It requires you to consider how often you have failed. It requires that you ask yourself how often, when courage was required, were you a coward? When persistence was required, did you give up? When commitment was required, did you lose faith? When it was time to stand on principle, did you fall down? Were you shortsighted when what was needed was vision? Your actions in life are part and parcel of your legacy. Now, failing does not, in and of itself, make you a failure. But your legacy will be one of failure if you don't learn from those failings and turn them into victories.

For generations, we prided ourselves on the impressive list of "firsts" by African Americans. But as the important "firsts" were exhausted, many of us ended our pursuits and abandoned the belief that there will always be some "first" to accomplish, and there will always be improvements to be made on those firsts. What if Venus and Serena Williams had decided that they didn't need to try very hard to win Wimbledon, since Althea Gibson had done it years before either of them drew their first breath? There were scores of great Black basketball players long before Michael Jordan came along, yet he still managed to set himself apart. Jesse Jackson, Sr., ran for president twice; so does that now mean no other Black person should run? Please.

Building a legacy begins with the simple understanding that a positive contribution is achievable. If you look at the condition of Black America and all the changes we have to make, it's clear why so many of us feel we can't leave anything of value behind. We will never change Black America if we don't change that attitude.

I doubt that many of us think, in a comprehensive way, about what we are doing specifically to make Black America better. When was the last time you were with your friends where the topic of conversation was what are we doing as a group to make Black America better? When was the last time you asked yourself, "What have I done today for the race?" I feel better when I have done the three E's: encouraged, enlightened, and empowered Black Americans. Every night when I go to bed, I review in my own mind what I did that particular day to make Black America better. I make it a daily ritual. It's the kind of ritual we all need if we are to make this part of our lives. Ask yourself: "Did I stop and speak to another Black person today? Did I write a letter to a particular newspaper, TV, or radio station to express an opinion? Did I write a note to tell someone I appreciate them or one of their good deeds?" How many of us go through an entire day without once telling our children we love them?

Part of establishing a legacy is living by principles to which you stick throughout your life. After all, the people we admire the most are those who stood on principle. You can't establish a sound legacy if you don't know what it is you believe.

In the final analysis, life for Black folks is like a heart monitor. It's going to go up and down. What you want to avoid is having that monitor flatline on you. The efforts among too many Blacks to make Black America better have flatlined. And many of us are standing around doing nothing, waiting for white people—or anybody, really—to show up with the defibrillators to shock us back to life. We do not have the luxury of continuing this practice. We have to resuscitate ourselves.

As Black Americans, we have to approach our legacies as if they are individual bricks in a wall. We cannot have a wall without those bricks and, without the wall, we're nothing but a mess of bricks waiting to be carted away. If you have a chance to examine the Great Wall of China closely, you'll see that the bricks, in and of themselves, are rather ordinary. But as a collective unit, those bricks are one of the world's greatest wonders—and the only man-made wonder visible from outer space. As individuals we need to be dedicated and diligent about our actions that represent us a race to the rest of the world. We are headed in that direction, but we won't get there unless everybody considers their own legacy. We don't need anyone contributing a flawed brick to our great Black American wall. So, what are you doing to deserve *your* place in the wall?

Part

II

What Leading African
Americans Have to Say
About How to Make
Black America Better

Susan L. Taylor

Each Other's Keeper

For uncounted centuries they lived from sea to shining sea. The Cherokee Nation, the Choctaw, Chickasaw, and Creek. The Iroquois, Navajo, Blackfeet, and Mohawk. The Hopi, Anishinabe, Shinnecock, Shawnee. . . .

Like our African ancestors, they were spiritual people, with complex institutions, fixed habits and tastes. People who didn't believe in individual ownership of the land, but respected and cherished it communally because it sustained them, held the bones of their ancestors. Like our African ancestors, they were dignified women and men, steady people, copper colored, and proud. They had no sheriffs, judges, or jails, but were governed by a strict sense of right and wrong. And just like our African ancestors, they welcomed their European visitors—not into an empty wilderness or uncharted jungle, but into ancient and organized worlds where fidelity to the family and clan was paramount, where women were respected and children cherished. In these ancient nations and kingdoms, relationships between individuals, clans, and tribes were more humane, more civilized, than in the culture of the Europeans who came under the guise of saving the soul of "savages," and went on to destroy both civilizations, with the Bible in one hand and a gun in the other.

We must look back to understand the catastrophic events of history that have shaped our lives so that we can reshape them going forward.

In the 1400s in Europe, gold, not land, became the measure of wealth, and the heads of the new European nation-states were financing expeditions to unknown shores to feed their ravenous hunger to find it. On October 12, 1492, Christopher Columbus, a merchant's clerk and expert sailor from Genoa, seeking an ocean route to Asia, happened upon an island in the Bahamas. The native people called themselves Arawaks. Their bodies decorated with gold, they swam out to welcome the visitors. Columbus and his men took the Arawaks prisoner and forced them to guide the crew to the source of the gold, Hispaniola, the Caribbean island that today is Haiti and the Dominican Republic. There, Columbus and his fellow sailors built a fort, the first military base in the Western Hemisphere. For the peoples of the Americas, Europe, and Africa, life would never again be the same.

All this is the well-documented truth about the beginnings of slavery in North America. But the history we were taught transposes the heroes and the villains. Historian Howard Zinn, in his masterwork, *A People's History of the United States,* gives us an accurate account, and he carefully and clearly documents it all. He tells how, when the Spaniards realized there were no gold fields in the region, to pay off the debt to the stockholders who had financed their expeditions, they began capturing and filling their ships with the native men, women, and children and selling them into slavery back in Spain. And millions of native people were forced into slavery on plantations in the Caribbean. All of this in the name of the Holy Trinity.

"Trying to put together an army of resistance," says Zinn, "the Arawaks faced Spaniards who had armor, muskets, swords, horses. When the Spaniards took prisoners they hanged them or burned them to death. Among the Arawaks, mass suicides began, with cassava poison. Infants were killed to save them from the Spaniards. In two years, through murder, mutilation, or suicide, half of the 250,000 Indians on Haiti were dead." By 1515 there were 50,000 native people left; by 1550, around 500; and by 1650, none.

The Europeans who arrived after Columbus built sugar plantations throughout the Caribbean, and later would build huge plantations to grow sugar, cotton, and tobacco here in the Colonies. These criminals attempted to enslave the native people wherever they found them but couldn't force them to work. The indigenous Americans were vulnerable as well to the many diseases that Europeans brought, and the violence they wrought. To build the plantation economies that over centuries created tremendous wealth throughout the Americas and in Europe, there was a critical need for labor. Africans were the answer. And so our ancestors were torn away from their kin, their land, and their culture—everything dear and familiar to their hearts.

In 1619 a ship of misery flying the Dutch flag docked at the British colony of Jamestown, Virginia. Among its cargo were twenty Africans, the first enslaved Black people in North America. By this time at least a million Africans were already in slavery on plantations owned by the Portuguese and Spanish throughout South and Central America and the Caribbean.

The Atlantic slave trade had begun in 1441 when Lancarote de Freitas, the Portuguese captain of a newly formed company for trade to Africa, found that "slaves were in more ample supply" than the gold the merchants of Lisbon had paid him and other sailors to find. These first expeditions carried the human cargo back to Portugal and the Portuguese islands, the Azores, and Madeira, before they began transporting Africans to Brazil in the early 1500s. Historians estimate that as many as 100 million people were stolen from the Continent and carried to Europe and the Americas between 1441 and 1886, when Cuba became the last colony in the Western Hemisphere to abolish slavery.

As many as 60 million Africans perished during the Middle Passage, or Maafa. There is "a railroad of bones" at the bottom of the Atlantic Ocean. Sharks learned to follow the slave ships because they knew they'd be fed. This odious act of people-stealing went on for 445 years. The question that lingers in my heart is: *How was this tolerated for so long?*

We have to look back, understand the events of history and how they have affected us psychologically, spiritually, and economically to be able to construct a new story.

In his epic document *The Slave Trade,* historian Hugh Thomas says this world-altering commercial undertaking not only involved millions of people but also every maritime European nation, every Atlantic-facing African people (and some others), and every country of the Americas. The late, great historian and prime minister of Trinidad, Dr. Eric Williams, has documented how the profits of the Liverpool slave traders financed the industrial revolution in England. The stock market, too, was created from the spoils of the lucrative slave trade. You don't even have to know how to count to understand what was built here over the centuries with a seemingly inexhaustible supply of free Black labor: the wealthiest country in the world, the United States of America.

These tragic and monumental episodes—the destruction of Native American civilization, the removal and massacre of millions of Native American people, and the enslavement of tens of millions of African people, which subsequently led to the destruction of Black civilization—are the deepest wounds in the soul of this nation. We must acknowledge them, deconstruct and deal with them so that all of us can heal.

The broken treaties say so much. The United States government signed more than 400 treaties with the native people—and violated every single one of them. The poverty that exists today in a nation so rich with natural resources, talent, and technology screams loudly—*30 million people go hungry here every day; 3 million are homeless. There is no name for this other than* genocide.

To make things better for ourselves, we must know what we are facing. To make things better for ourselves, we must understand the American way, an ingenious system of control driven by the politics of greed. We must understand the mess we're in before we can mend it, before we can become a people united for foundational change.

We need to look back at the truth of our experience so we will *know* that we are not inferior or incomplete in any way, and that we *can* make Black America, this country, and the world a better place.

I look back so that I never forget the enormity of our loss and our suffering and the ways they have sapped our energy. The wonder is not that so many brothers and sisters have lost their way or perished. The wonder is that despite the barbarous acts of violence rendered for more than six centuries, so many have survived. History reveals that no other people who have suffered so much remain in existence.

We are who we are, if we are anybody, says minister and scholar Dr. Renita Weems, because some Black person stooped low enough to allow us to climb on and ride piggyback into the future.

How can we today make Black America better? What must we do on our watch? These are the critical questions each of us should pose to ourselves at this pivotal time in our history.

All that is happening around us, all that is disturbing and painful in our communities, is a reflection of our collective consciousness. There has been a fateful split of flesh from Spirit, and, consequently, on some level we're all suffering; we all feel alone. In our isolation, ironically, we are one with humanity. Most of us are afraid there isn't enough on the planet to go around, that we will never attain as much as we desire. For African Americans to heal, we must face the truth: We've come to believe that material wealth will quench our longing for happiness. It will not. Envy and longing, greed and exploitation—these are the underpinnings of Western culture, and some of the system's empty values have rubbed off on us.

We are each other's keeper. The wise poet laureate of Illinois, Gwendolyn Brooks, says that we are each other's harvest and each other's business:

We are each other's magnitude and bond.

A strong and errant group is standing in the way of Black progress, and it is us. The central problem for African Americans—and for Black people throughout the world—is unity. This has been our problem historically. Today there is still little sense of kinship among the different tribes of African peoples. When our African ancestors began selling prisoners of war into slavery, they looked upon their brethren with hatred, saw them as aliens whose destiny was of no concern. Over the centuries, the fragmentation and disunity in Africa has been cataclysmic. Africans warring against Africans has led to the devastation of our race. "The Blacks, as usual, were too busy fighting among themselves to mark the heralds of their doom or see the significance of the [European exploring expeditions]," says Chancellor Williams in his pioneering research and appraisal of the Black experience, *The Destruction of Black Civilization: Great Issues of a Race from 4500 B.C. to 2000 A.D.*

We are each other's keeper. Everything and everyone on God's good earth is interconnected and has to be thought of as a whole. All that exists coexists. This is the simple yet difficult lesson the Creator has been trying to teach humanity—and First People, Black people—for eons. *Love thy neighbor as thyself,* for all of us together belong to a harmony, a community that is dependent, interdependent, on love. The love and understanding we need for our personal healing is also needed to heal our community, this country, and the larger world. Love. It is the ultimate authority over all the forces in the world. Love. It vanquishes all obstacles and obstructions.

We will give birth to a structure and a new age as loving-kindness becomes our way. The revered minister and author Marianne Williamson sums it up well: Racial tension, decivilization of our cities, violence and drugs among our youth and in our neighborhoods, economic disparity between rich and poor, global strife—the most serious problems we face as a nation are not actually solvable through traditional political means because they are the wounds of an internal disease.

The way to our healing is within. The most revolutionary act you and I can practice at this moment is to love and trust our true selves fiercely, and vow fidelity to one another. We must believe in ourselves, in one another, and in the possibilities for healing and transformation. Love and faith must be alive and deeply rooted within us. These are our sustaining power. Look at the history; look all around us today. Whenever, wherever we forsake these spiritual principles that are at the center of all the world's great religious faiths, things fall apart. In the words of Audre Lorde, how can we build a nation if we're afraid to speak out, afraid to walk out into the moonlight?

Fear is our only enemy. Fear is the source of all the needless suffering in the world. How do we in our day-to-day living love ourselves, love one another, and fear nothing? The answers to these vital questions provide the foundation and guiding light for our healing and the healthy future we all want to create. Whether we call our Creator God, Allah, Jehovah, or Spirit, this is what we have come to this life to learn.

What happens on our watch dictates the future for our people. The hardest work has been done by the generations before us. Here are a few things that *we* must do.

Attend to Our Emotional Well-Being

We have to know what is and isn't working in our lives so that we can heal what is hurting us. Commit to therapy, to doing your inner work, your soul work. Find healthy vents for your emotions—running, walking, laughing, shouting by the water, if that's what it takes. Do whatever you must to restore and maintain your emotional well-being.

Beloved, this is the most critical piece of life's puzzle, for as we become emotionally whole, we prosper in every area of our lives.

We have clarity, giving us the ability to make the best decisions for ourselves and one another. When we love and honor ourselves, when we have a full cup, we're not hungry and foolish in love, and we do not tolerate disrespect. We show up for ourselves—at the doctor, the gym, in the policy-making and political arenas. We nourish body and soul; we stop placing undue stress on ourselves. We pay our bills on time and speak kindly to our children; our money gets straight, our divine-right mate appears—everything in our lives swings into balance. It's God's promise: *Seek ye first the kingdom, and everything you want will be given to you.*

The best thing you can do for yourself, your family, and Black America is attend to your wholeness each and every day. Then you will bring your love and joy—the healing balm—with you wherever you go. As you are healed, you heal others, your family, our community.

Have Zero Tolerance for Violence

A piece of our soul died the day that some brothers broke into Rosa Parks's home and beat her up. Draw the line. Make it unacceptable—and dangerous—to brutalize our women, our elders, or any person.

Make Getting an Education Hip and Cool Again

Let's make learning exciting and fun, and let's be respectful of our learning differences. We have to meet our kids in crisis where they are: Stick your nose in the business of an underserved school where our children are failing, and work with others at shaping a curriculum that values Black culture and experience. Work toward making teachers among the highest-paid people in our society, and hold them accountable to the highest standards and goals. Make it possible for motivated, skilled Black teachers to come through the system, and then reward them for teaching in our most challenging schools. And for yourself? Make new learning your lifetime commitment.

Be Aware of the Prison Industry

The prison system is a business, and it's among the most profitable industries in the nation. Black, Latino, and Native American young people—in failing schools and crazed by the drugs we allow in our communities and the violence we allow in the media—have become the fodder feeding the system. The prison industry is being privatized and is using our tax dollars to build jails in rural communities, far away from us, making jobs available to the folks who live there. Black men are 5 percent of the population and 50 percent of the inmates. In your place of worship and community, put incarceration issues high on the agenda.

We must enter the prisons, give these brothers and sisters love, and help them cure their addictions. We have to turn these holding pens into places of learning, with tried-and-true educational and values-training programs. My husband, Khephra Burns, says the ticket out of the joint should be a Ph.D.

Support Activist Organizations and Institutions

Identify at least one local and national organization that is effectively working on the critical issues affecting our community, and become involved. Attend meetings, assist in fund-raising and program development, and hold the leadership responsible for achieving measurable results.

Sisters, don't pray where you can't preach. Brothers, retire your sexist attitudes. It's as difficult to get some brothers to check their wounding sexist ways as it is to get some White folks to check their wounding racist attitudes.

Embrace Difference

Remember the lesson we were created to learn: We are all one, each other's keeper, regardless of the accent flowing from our tongue, how we choose to worship, or with whom we choose to partner. There's a very strong, activist, and monied Black gay community that wants in, that wants to help our people. As a group, we've been homophobic and have made only a small space at the table for our gay brothers, those whose creative energy we rely on. Open wide your mind and heart and invite our gay brothers and lesbian sisters, whom we've totally shunned, to the banquet. We need all our strengths to leverage our liberation.

Be Love, Be Peace

Watch your mind and mind your mouth. Be the watchperson at the gate each moment, and try to make everything you think, say, and do positive. Then you will live your highest potential. Then you needn't go to the temple to worship, because the temple will be your heart—and your life your prayer.

Cathy Hughes

History, Heritage, and Hope

History is what has happened to us in the past. *Heritage* is what, in the present, we understand about our history. *Hope* is what we give to the future based upon what has happened to us in the past and what we understand about that experience. It was important for other groups to deny our history in order to make us misunderstand our heritage and thereby eliminate our ability to produce the hope that is so necessary for future generations. They were *almost* successful.

It was important for those in power to make it seem as though our history began with slavery instead of 4.5 million years ago. By doing so, the entire process of our achievement was severed from restoring ourselves to our own former glory and tied only to becoming equal to theirs. It *almost* worked.

It was important to make us believe that we had no substance and that our only hope lay in being linked to their progress. That is how we were so subtly shifted from desegregation to integration. And many of us fell for it.

We, for the most part, have been fooled to settle for simple access. Somehow we were convinced that freedom equaled having access to someone else's dream or to being a walk-on in someone else's Broadway play. Somewhere along the line, we were convinced that all of the struggles of Black people were accomplished in order that we may see ourselves, our generation, as the culmination of all of the history of African people on this continent. America wants us to believe that we "have arrived"—that the revolution is over. I ask you this, "Now that we have 'arrived,' just where the hell are we? Where do we go from here, and how do we get there?"

We now stand at the doorway of the twenty-first century. Through this portal we see that God has given us a new mind, a new spirit, and a new life. We have been born again as Africans living in America. As such, let us shake ourselves out of the smoke and mirrors of the American hallucination. Let us turn away from the fabrications that rob our communities of the cohesion and success we deserve. Let us recognize, once again, that until all of us succeed, truly none of us is standing on a foundation worthy of our effort. It is easy to eat up all of the resources or to wear them on our backs, but that is not how we got here and that is not how we shall go from here. To whom much is given, much is REQUIRED! Mary McLeod left a legacy, Martin left a dream, Malcolm left a challenge, and Sojourner left truth. What shall we leave?

We must serve as the vanguard that will stimulate and pilot our people to economic, spiritual, educational, and communal empowerment. We can begin empowering our community by reclaiming the responsibility for defining our cultural focus. As a people, we must say which images can and cannot be tolerated. We need to impose acceptable limits on how our people may be portrayed by ourselves and by others. We should determine, within the bounds of our community, what is considered correct and what is not permissible. Our definition of ourselves must be clear and consistent; and we must be willing to marshal all of our strength to ensure that we are afforded the same respect that all others demand.

Empowering our community also requires reconceptualizing our place in the world. While we, Africans living in America, may be a minority population within the borders of the United States, we are but a small portion of a vast world African population. On this planet, only Africans and Chinese number in excess of 1 billion people. We are not a minority, and should not be limited to doing business in America. The entire world should be seen as our market arena. We must reject any language or definition that limits our achievement and robs our community of the benefits of creation and success.

Today, the conventional thinking is that Black people need "role models." The concept of a "role model" presupposes, however, that there is no collective, intrinsic standard of Black behavior. Furthermore, it says that there are only a few "chosen" individuals worthy of imitation. In reality, we do have a collective standard of excellence, and that spiritual, incredibly wonderful standard of behavior is over 100 years old.

Black people do not need role models; we need to help ourselves return to our collective standard of decency, honesty, hard work, sharing, caring, and reaching back. When success is based on the motivation of a role model, the entire system of reference is open to destruction based simply upon the possible failure of the role model—that one person. When we aspire, however, to the higher collective standard, no single failure can damage or cause the individual to lose hope. A personal failure is brought back to redemption by aligning the person once again to the collective standard.

Something in our cultural arsenal must be the fuel to move us from the dark and confusing present into a brighter and clearer tomorrow. A future-seeking message can pave the way in darkness. Many of our youth, however, have no concept of a future-seeking message. As adults, we must guide and support our young people. We must provide the skills that will help them fashion a positive message. We must help them transform their raw and unshaped talent into productive careers. We must prepare them to take up the struggle and do their part in the advancement of Black people. We must spend more time talking with them and less time talking about them. Finally, we must spend more time training them and less time blaming them.

It is not just the young who need support. We must devise ways of assisting each other in the process of empowerment. For example, we all need goods and services. If we buy those goods and services from a source outside of our community, the benefit of our dollars will not go into our community. To the extent, however, that we purchase those goods and services from within our community, those dollars will recirculate, building strength and funding for the future of our communities.

Another way to achieve empowerment is to assist every sister and brother with whom we come in contact by enabling them to see the potential for business in the things that they would gladly do for free. We have many models before us. Our grandmothers took the small things that they did well and utilized them to keep our mothers and fathers in college. Small baking and auto repair businesses provided the stash that many of our elder mothers, aunts, and uncles kept down in those corsets, brassieres, and tin cans. What we have done independently and somewhat haphazardly in the past, I am now calling for us to structure and to plan. This can spell the difference between a peoplehood that survives and thrives and one that disappears.

Let me turn briefly to our history and its implications. African people, by and large, have lost or surrendered our collective memory of others—and ourselves—and accepted false ones in their place. As African people, our struggle has been dreadfully bitter though "brief." Please do not miss my point. Our suffering, which the African scholars call the "Maafa," has been devastating because of the total viciousness of our tormentors. My point is this: Slavery, devastation, and depression was not our beginning, and slavery, devastation, and depression will not be our end. In the context of nearly 5 million years here on the planet, the last 500 has been brief.

We must understand this fact of history in order to devise an *agenda* that will bring our suffering to an end. There are two tendencies in history: that which is being born and coming into being, and that which is dying and coming to an end. What determines what will be born and what will die in many cases is the will of the people concerned. The will of a people comes into fruition when there is a plan or an agenda in place.

For example, it is a fact that every group immigrating to this country was despised and made to operate in a second-class fashion. Each of these groups recognized, however, that they needed a plan. The Irish found their salvation by launching a concerted effort to infiltrate the police departments, which had previously arrested so many Irishmen that it became appropriate to nickname the jail wagon after the diminutive and derogatory form of the popular Irish name, "Patrick," hence the paddy wagon. The Italians within a few generations, backed up by their internal-external police force, moved to control the major trade unions and to build a large property development business to launder monies made in the street trades. The Jews began as peddlers of small cheap jewelry items and rags, and in the early 1900s, were said to be too dumb to be accepted into the military services. Within three generations, they built an empire by moving from rags to fabrics and from fabrics to clothing. Finally, they shifted from clothing to corner the market on the development of major department stores. At the same time, they put a high premium in their community on the development of physicians and attorneys. Asian immigrants targeted the area of food, utilizing their entry as small market owners to manipulate themselves into controlling food warehousing and food distribution.

Each of these communities solved their problems by creating a multigenerational plan. More serious than our "having a problem" has been our inability to *understand* how to solve our problem. We African Americans have demonstrated that we are very good at making short-distance runs. In the Olympics and in life, we have mastered the 100-yard dash. Unfortunately, life is not a short dash. Life is a distance sport. And we have not done very well making long-term runs. Therefore, we must put our collective minds together to construct the plan that we shall deliver to our babies over the next several generations.

This plan should be based, in part, on our traditions. Recall that each of us has come to this place in our lives, across the rivers and streams of danger, lifted by people who guided and protected us. We are not "the ends" of this process of sharing. Helping, caring, and sharing are integral parts of a never-ending process, as our African ancestors correctly understood. We must remember that African society is community based. Each person takes his understanding of their existence from the fact that they are part of a community. René Descartes, the seventeenth-century French philosopher, is credited with the phrase *"Cogito, ergo sum,"* meaning "I think, therefore I am." Descartes defined his existence in terms of his ability to *think;* however, my African foreparents expressed their understanding of existence in this way, *"I am, because you are."*

My African approach grounds me firmly in the duty and responsibility that is consistent with my experience. This experience tells me that all that I have, or will ever have, is of value only in terms of what I can do with it to assist others. To an African, having all of the gold and treasures of the universe and being alone is a curse worse than death. I share this in hopes of illuminating our vision of what we are and what we can be. *"I am because you are, and you are because we are."*

Furthermore, within the African tradition it is said that in the village there is no word for "alone." This reinforces the concept of community. We are here to form small cooperative villages; some may call them neighborhoods or communities. We must take into our villages the young babies who are yearning for an understanding of life. We must help form the values, set the sights, raise the expectations, and supply the skills needed to make their goals achievable. There is a feeling of satisfaction and fulfillment derived from providing a future for those whose future is in doubt. This is the purpose of our existence.

I began with a discussion of history, heritage, and hope, and so I will end with this final thought: Between every car in a train there is a linchpin. The linchpin joins the front car to the one that is next behind. It is not the strength of the front car that pulls the back car. It is the strength of the linchpin, which joins the first to the last. Do you see? Our *history* has been strong and deserves a future. Our *hope* is great and needs a pull from the past. History, however, does not touch hope without *heritage*. History cannot touch hope unless we stand as the linchpin, joining past to future. That is our calling!

How We, as African Americans, Can Improve Our Community and Our Country in the Twenty-first Century

D r. W. E. B. Du Bois, in his classic book *The Souls of Black Folk*, made the perceptive observation that "The problem of the twentieth century is the problem of the color line. . . ." Unfortunately, that problem will probably be just as acute in the twenty-first century. We, as a people, confronted it in the twentieth century with protests, mass demonstrations, moral persuasion, prayers, litigation, politics, cultural assertiveness, and, on rare occasions, boycotts.

What is conspicuously missing from that list is consistent, serious, sophisticated, selective use of our enormous economic potential. I deliberately use the word "potential" because rarely in the past have we successfully maximized our collective economic clout as a weapon in the ongoing struggle for equal rights, equal opportunity, and equal justice. With due respect to the honorable Rosa Parks and the Montgomery bus boycott, we too often ignore the salient fact that it was the use of collective economic power that brought that situation to a successful conclusion.

African Americans in Montgomery stopped riding the buses; since Black patronage was absolutely critical to the company's profits, it was eventually forced into bankruptcy. They acknowledged the power of collective economic clout when they sued Mrs. Parks, charging her with forcing their company out of business. It wasn't the rhetoric, the preaching, the belief that right was on our side that moved the white supremacists to action; it was the cold-blooded fact of Black folks' effective use of collective economic power. It was a splendid example that we, unfortunately, failed to develop as the ultimate weapon in our quest for first-class citizenship. For instance, if a bank refuses to provide loans for Black customers, there's no need for weeping and wailing, moaning and groaning, empty rhetoric, or loud, meaningless threats. All that has to be done is for one thousand Black individuals and institutions to stop by that bank and remove their money. That, quicker and more effectively than anything else, would grab the attention of bank executives in the entire industry.

Our collective economic clout is a powerful weapon in our money-driven society. Our neglect of using it in the latter half of the twentieth century severely impeded our progress, politically, economically, culturally, and educationally. We must enter the new century with a new strategy and a new attitude, one that declares that where our dignity is dishonored, our dollars will be withheld; where our humanity is disrespected, our dollars will be redirected. We are the descendants of courageous ancestors who not only survived unprecedented physical and psychological brutality but actually built successful institutions under extremely hostile conditions. Instead of lamenting our past and present flaws and failures, we must spend our valuable time identifying, analyzing, and documenting the strengths of our ancestors and of ourselves and focus on developing ways to build on them.

African Americans' collective economy is equal to the twelfth-largest economy in the world. A group of people who spend over $427 billion annually in a money-driven society should be a major player in financial and other markets of the nation. Should this be our destiny in the twenty-first century, it will truly be one for the ages.

Making Black America Better

I am a Black woman, wife, mother, grandmother, and an elected representative. I represent the 35th Congressional District in the U.S. House of Representatives. I take my responsibility seriously, and while I am, indeed, elected by the voters of the 35th District in California, I use my office as a platform and forum to address the needs and concerns of the African diaspora.

I am obsessed with the question "How to make Black America better." The Black America of which I speak is not a geographic consideration. It is not a Black America narrowly defined as the hood or the ghetto. Black America is linked by the consciousness of a people who have come this far, snatched from their native land, shackled with the chains of slavery, despised, cursed, denounced, and denied the common courtesies of human recognition. Yet, we have survived, competed, and progressed. We are winners; however, we have not yet won all that we will win. We must demand respect, resist discrimination, insist on our fair share of everything—educational opportunities, economic parity, jobs, business ownership, political leadership, access to capital—and understand the basic right to realize our full potential using our God-given talent and access to opportunity and fair treatment.

We have been on this journey—the quest for freedom, justice, and equality—for a long time, and the memory of our history is fading with each new generation. The griot is gone—the history books rewritten and the elders silenced with government hot-lunch programs, new senior-citizen buildings, and the trips to Las Vegas. Too many Black ministers compete to build the biggest and prettiest cathedrals, with a message on Sunday mornings taken from a prescribed text from the Christian Coalition. At their yearly banquets, the nonprofits representing the civil rights movement honor the very bankers and leaders of financial institutions who are responsible for predatory lending and redlining our communities. The tobacco industry, which laser-beams their advertisements to our young people and helps foster sickness and death, underwrites "community" activities. Community leaders and politicians often give plaques and commendations to the very people who market "40"-ounce poison to our children. Too many politicians take money from the very corporate interests that are opposed to public policy support for the poor and are also opposed to affirmative action and civil rights.

Far too many mothers and fathers cannot fight against crack cocaine in our communities. Too many are "cracked out," languishing in a prison system especially designed for African Americans, which guarantees they will help keep it full with foolish acts of petty crime. The criminal justice system uses these offenses as excuses to "lock them up and throw away the key." The prison-industrial complex is thriving on the backs of our precious men and boys and, increasingly, our mothers and grandmothers.

"How to make Black America better?" Every home, every barbershop, every beauty shop, more Saturday schools, every church, every social club—sororities and fraternities—must adopt a plan to teach, to instill, to train Black people how to love themselves and each other. Everything begins with belief in self. When one believes in self, one is empowered to improve one's family and community. That we are Black, competent, and capable must be our mantra.

Success in our pursuit of justice is absolutely dependent on the belief that we can and will make it happen. It is in our hands. It is in our power.

This knowledge of strength and power will propel us to take control of where we live. Clean up, paint up, wash up, and scrub up—cleanliness is next to godliness. If government will not sweep our streets, empty our garbage, clean our alleys, we will! We will mobilize our community to take on city hall and force them to provide the services. When our surroundings are in order, our minds can be clearer and better organized. When we know who we are and reach back to the words of our foreparents who told us to "Go to school, get an education; they cannot take what's inside your head," we will know that we must demand the best education, petition the boards of education to waive silly and restricting rules. We must create an education agenda, get involved in evaluating and rating teachers, principals, and administrators. We cannot allow schools to continue to deteriorate in our communities, and we must organize and attend school board meetings and visit the schools. Whether you have a child in the school system or not is of no consequence. Our children represent our future.

The big question for Black America is "Are we going to share in the economic possibilities of this nation?" We are great consumers. We buy every new gimmick, cosmetic, automobile, and item of designer wear put before us. It is time to force corporate America to enter into joint ventures, give more foundation support to new technology opportunities, and purchase from Black businesses. It is time for well-planned, well-organized boycotts. We have got to make believers out of corporate interests who are milking us and our communities.

If we join our economic strength and our political strength, we can make Black America better. Every Black person must register and vote. Every Black person must know his or her elected official. Every Black person must learn to write a letter of complaint or support, attend a meeting, join an organization, call a radio station, organize a block club, support a Saturday school, get involved—get active!

We can be proud of the progress we have made, but we can do better. We can make Black America better. We need but understand the power is in our hands. Change will not come from the exploiters, the "do-gooders," or the observers of it all. Change starts inside.

It works its way into the way you see life.

It wrestles with injustice.

It confronts unfairness.

It deals with obstacles.

It demands truth and resolution.

We will make Black America better when we start with ourselves!

Johnnie L. Cochran, Jr.

Controlling Our Destinies

We need a concerted effort in the Black community to reemphasize the importance of education, because knowledge is power. Not power to dominate others, but power to control our own destinies.

Our lot in America is inextricably tied to our preparation and education. I see the new civil rights frontier as seeking economic empowerment on behalf of all African Americans in the twenty-first century. Each one of us deserves an opportunity to go as far as our talent and ability will allow us without being held back because of race, creed, color, or gender. Although most of us weren't raised on Wall Street, there's no reason we cannot move into that neighborhood now as we look to the future.

We also need to continue efforts to eradicate racism in so many of our institutions, and to continue to fight insidious racial profiling that permeates too many segments of our society.

And finally, we need to return to our spiritual roots for nourishment and guidance as we seek to put our hands in the unchanging hands of God. We need to realize that all things are possible if we trust in God, and believe that the best is yet to come.

Henry Louis Gates, Jr.

Hard Truths

Everyone knows there are two nations in this country, white and Black, right? That's what the Kerner Commission Report said in 1968, and that's what the title of Andrew Hacker's bestselling sequel to that report says today. And for good reason. Track the statistics for public health, educational attainment, and income, and they all seem to point to the same thing: that African Americans are the ultimate unassimilables of the American mix, the pebble in the ethnic soup.

Peer a little closer, though, and this familiar image splits again. Even as the ranks of the underclass expand, a second nation-within-a-nation has formed. The fact is, Afro-America's affluent elite is larger than it has ever been—a legacy of the post–civil rights era and just the kind of corporate and governmental programs of intervention that have fallen into such disfavor of late.

Now, most of the Black communities' leaders, self-appointed or otherwise, are loath to acknowledge the existence of this class. They take it as part of their role to publicize the dire condition afflicting so much of Black America. Why distract from the real problem? But here's the rub. Opponents of these post–civil rights era programs can then flatly declare that they have failed.

How to explain the complicated truth that for Black America, these are the worst of times . . . and the best of times?

Today many Black Americans enjoy a measure of economic security beyond any we have known in the history of Black America. But if they remain in a nasty blue funk, it's because their very existence seems an affront to the swelling ranks of the poor. Nor have Black intellectuals ever quite made peace with the concept of the Black bourgeoisie, a group that is typically seen as devoid of cultural authenticity, doomed to mimicry and pallid assimilation. I once gave a talk before an audience of Black academics and educators, in the course of which I referred to Black middle-class culture. Afterward, one of the academics in the audience, deeply affronted, had a question for me. "Professor Gates," he asked rhetorically, his voice dripping with sarcasm, "what is Black middle-class culture?" I suggested that if he really wanted to know, he need only look around the room. But perhaps I should just have handed him a mirror; for just as nothing is more American than anti-Americanism, nothing is more characteristic of the Black bourgeoisie than the sense of shame and denial that the identity inspires. What did we do to be so black and blue? You may well ask.

The truth is that Black America has always been uncomfortable with the fact of its divisions, and none more so than the members of the middle class.

What do we do about this? What do we not do? First of all, it's time for the Black middle class to stop feeling guilty about its own success while fellow Blacks languish in the inner city of despair. Black prosperity does not derive from Black poverty. Those who succeed are those whose community, whose families, *prepared* them to be successful. As Stanley Crouch and others remind us, the familiar exhortation in those days was to "get all the education that you can"—and we did. When I left home for Yale, virtually my whole hometown celebrated. "The community," as we put it, however sentimentally, wished us to succeed. Talking Black, walking Black, wearing kente cloth, listening to Black music, and filling our walls with Black art—as desirable as these things can be in and of themselves—are not essential to "being Black." You can love Mozart, Picasso, and ice hockey and still be as Black as the ace of spades.

Second, we don't have to fail in order to be Black. As crazy as this sounds, recent surveys of young Black kids reveal a distressing pattern. Far too many say that succeeding is "white," education is "white," aspiring and dreaming are "white," believing that you can make it is "white." Had any of us said this sort of thing when we were growing up, our families and friends would have checked us into a mental institution. We need *more success* individually and collectively, not less.

Third, we don't have to pretend any longer that 30 million people can ever possibly be members of the same social class. After all, the entire population of Canada is 26 million. Canadians are not all members of one economic class. Nor do they speak with one single voice of one single leader. We have *never* been members of a single social or economic class, and never will be.

How do we "fight the power" in a post–civil rights world in which Bull Connors and George Wallace are no longer the easy targets that white racists used to be? A world in which the rhetoric of the civil rights era sounds tired and empty? (If someone had turned up at the Million Family March and handed over a check for $500 billion to heal the ills of the inner city, I wonder if anyone there would have known what to do with it.)

The time has come for honesty within the Black community.

The causes of poverty within the Black community are *both* structural and behavioral, as scholars as diverse as philosopher Cornel West and sociologist William Julius Wilson have insisted, and as most polemicists still shy from acknowledging. A generation of well-meaning social scientists has made the notion of "the culture of poverty" taboo, correctly observing that the concept as originally introduced ignored the economic and structural dimensions of the problem. But having acknowledged those dimensions, it's time to concede that, yes, there is a culture of poverty. How could there not be? How could you think that culture *matters* and deny its relation to economic success? In general, a household made up of a sixteen-year-old mother, a thirty-two-year-old grandmother, and a forty-eight-year-old great-grandmother is not a site for hope and optimism. It's also true that not everyone in any society wants to work, that not all people are equally motivated.

There! Was that so hard to say?

Our task, it seems to me, is to lobby for those social programs that have been demonstrated to make a difference for those sufficiently motivated to seize these expanded opportunities. More important, we have to demand a structural change in this country. We have to take people off welfare and train them for occupations relevant to a twenty-first-century economy. And while I'm sympathetic to such incentives as tax breaks to generate new investment in inner cities, youth apprenticeships with corporations, expanded tax credits for earned income, and tenant ownership of inner-city property, I believe we will have to face a reality. The reality is that our inner cities are not going to become oases of economic prosperity and corporate investment, and we should probably think about moving Black inner-city workers *to the jobs* rather than wait for new factories to resettle in the inner city.

To continue to repeat the same old stale formulas—to blame, in exactly the same way, "the man" for oppressing us all, to scapegoat Koreans, Jews, or even Haitians for seizing local entrepreneurial opportunities that have, for whatever reason, eluded us—is to fail to accept moral leadership. Not to demand that each member of the Black community accept individual responsibility for their behavior—whether that behavior assumes the form of gang violence, unprotected sexual activity, you name it—is another way of selling out a beleaguered community. It is to surrender to the temptation to act as ethnic cheerleaders "selling wolf tickets"—engaging in hollow rhetoric—from the suburbs instead of speaking the hard truths that may be unpopular with our fellows. Du Bois dared to speak an uncomfortable truth when he addressed the responsibilities of the Black elite. For them, the challenge awaits of healing the rift within Black America, and the larger nation as well.

The Freedom Symphony's Fourth Movement

We know the first three movements of our Freedom Symphony. The First Movement was the struggle to end slavery with its clash of ideas, of vision, of arms, and the drumbeat of armies. The Second was the struggle to end legal segregation, the trumpets of freedom's struggle, the clarion call of Dr. King's summons to sacrifice. The Third Movement featured the firm beat of marching feet climaxing with all Americans gaining the right to vote.

Now we must compose the Fourth Movement of the Freedom Symphony. It is the most complex, the hardest to compose, and the one for which the others were but prelude. It is the movement begun by Dr. King just before his death. This is the struggle to provide shared economic security and justice in the land.

It has many refrains—the need to provide a healthy start for all of God's children, the struggle for equal access to education, for investment in the promise of the young. It is the fight for health care for every American. It features a trumpet call for opening up access to capital, for greenlining the regions that have been redlined—from the South Side of Chicago to the Mississippi Delta and the Appalachian Hills.

This Fourth Movement represents a shift in how we think and

how we act, a shift from the race gap to the resource gap, the access to capital gap, from the horizontal struggle for equal rights to the vertical struggle for economic justice. This is the unfinished movement of Dr. King. He knew that a multiethnic, multi cultural campaign for economic justice had to be the final movement for the civil rights struggle. He knew that we had to move beyond voting rights and public accommodations to build a majority movement with a majority vision, one that challenged not only our public officials, but our private institutions—the corporate boardrooms, the suites of investment bankers, the offices of pension fund managers. We had to move from Edmund Pettis Bridge to Wall Street, LaSalle Street, and Silicon Valley.

But Dr. King's campaign was derailed. He was assassinated marching with sanitation workers organizing for a union in Memphis. Then the War on Poverty was lost to Vietnam, to Watergate, to Ronald Reagan, to the Cold War. A quarter century of conservative reaction first created deficits and then demanded paying off all debt. Deferred, disdained, derailed—until now.

So what is the one initiative that should be the centerpiece of this Fourth Movement? First, we must save the children: prenatal care and nutrition for mothers, health care for children, universal head start and preschool, universal child care, star schools for all, after-school and summer school programs.

"Leave no child behind." That's the slogan of the Children's Defense Fund. We do a shamefully poor job of meeting this injunction. Almost one in five children grow up in poverty. We do less to lift them up than any other industrial nation. In cities, our infant mortality rates are worse than those in Cuba. Preschool education is not available. Our public schools suffer from a "savage inequality." Some kids hurdle the universal tests with boosters on their feet; others hurdle them with shackles on their legs. There is neither moral justification nor political excuse for this.

This is not simply a government program. When I grew up, I was encompassed by a triangle of love—home, church, and school—to lift me when I fell and catch me when I strayed. Too often today, each point of that triangle is now weakened. So in our commitment to children, we must seek to rebuild the family, to reduce the number of babies having babies, to ensure that schools are small enough to know what's going on and active enough to care. Churches, community groups, faith-based institutions—as they are now called—must play an active role in saving the young.

But public investment is crucial. It is simply shameful that we do not ensure that every child gets a healthy start, attends an exciting school, and has opportunity opened to him or her.

We know that prenatal care can dramatically lower the risk of premature, low-weight, or at-risk babies. Yet we do not ensure prenatal care for all mothers. We know that infant nutrition is vital to mental development and proper growth. Yet too many still face hunger at night. We know that the brain develops rapidly at an early age. But preschool is generally unavailable and unaffordable. We know that children are greatly influenced by the schools they attend. Yet too many schools send the message that we don't expect much of them, that they are second-class children.

There is no excuse. For a long time, these programs went without funding because our focus was on the Cold War. Then, as the Cold War ended, we faced staggering budget deficits, and deficit reduction took priority. Now the United States has no military rival. We witness budget surpluses "as far as the eye can see." Inequality has grown to obscene extremes. There is no excuse.

Investing in children is, of course, only one refrain of the Fourth Movement. We need to bring capital to those areas that have been redlined. We can challenge Wall Street on its own terms. Rural and urban America has what investors seek: underserved markets, underutilized talent, and untapped capital. We have markets, money, talent, location, ability, will to work, and a patriot's claim.

This market numbers more than 60 million people. It commands more than $600 billion in annual earnings. Compared to the world's economies, it would rank fifteenth, ahead of Mexico, Switzerland, Indonesia, and India. It is more accessible than these, more stable, closer to airports and highways. It is growing in economic prowess every year. It is time to open up these untapped markets. To bring capital to the areas that have been redlined. Already we have made progress. Our work on the Wall Street Project has been turned into a presidential initiative. I was proud to accompany President Clinton on his tour across America for the New Markets Initiative. Building a bridge from Wall Street to Appalachia, from Wall Street to the Delta, from Wall Street to Harlem—that is part of our new journey. But it is only a part.

Just as we must build the bridge to Wall Street and engage private capital, we must change our public priorities to invest public capital in education and health care, in head start and child care, in affordable housing, clean water, and clean air. We need a government that stands for labor rights and environmental protections across the world so that this new global marketplace works to lift people up, not drive them down in a race to the bottom. Private capital is necessary; public investment is vital.

For all this to succeed, we have to make up our minds and act. In our lifetime, change has never come from the White House down. It comes from the people up. Kennedy did not have civil rights on his agenda; Dr. King and the civil rights movement made integration inescapable. Lyndon Johnson said he couldn't get the Voting Rights Act through Congress. It was the Selma March and the sacrifice and efforts of millions that won voting rights for all.

And now, the Fourth Movement of the Freedom Symphony will be composed from the bottom up, or it will not be written at all. For that to happen, African Americans have to change the way we look at the world, and at ourselves. "And we saw the giants, the sons of Anak, which come of the giants, and we were in our own sight as grasshoppers, and so we were in their sight." The quotation comes from the Old Testament, but similar passages can be found in every religion. We cannot be big and little at the same time. If we see others as giants and ourselves as grasshoppers, so others shall see us.

You can't get majority answers asking minority questions. You can't get major blessings praying minor prayers. We must see ourselves through a big door, not through a tiny keyhole. A grasshopper's vision is limited; its horizons are small. We must see ourselves as giants, with vision enough for an entire nation, not just one part of it.

Dr. King was a Black minister in the segregated South. But his vision and his courage made him a world leader. Today they sing *We Shall Overcome* in China, Poland, Indonesia, Africa, and Nicaragua. His words, his dream, incite passion and foster hope across the globe.

The Bible says we shall be transformed by the renewal of our minds. We are giants, not grasshoppers—and if we allow ourselves to aim high enough, to look far enough, and to work hard enough, we can renew our minds and transform our world.

The historic refrains of the Fourth Movement of the Freedom Symphony will only resound when we lift our sights and our spirits and make our own music.

Nikki Giovanni

Rising Just a Bit Higher

There are many good things that have happened in this century: People all over the globe have struck blows for freedom following the pattern of the American civil rights movement led by African Americans. We are rightfully proud of that. And what an irony that *Plessy* v. *Ferguson,* a train situation, became the ultimate rallying cry that would make America better. Wouldn't it have been wonderful if Plessy had won and the United States had gone on to build better public transportation systems both interstate and intrastate? Instead of old people driving well past the time that they are capable and the rest of us battling trucks and traffic on a crumbling highway system, we all could be sitting in a clean, comfortable club car on a train, having a beer and spotting wildlife on our way home from work. Black America should feel proud to continue chipping at and chopping down white racism. With each challenge to our community we rise just a bit higher.

E. Lynn Harris

Cherished

When we think about how we can make our community better and stronger, cheerleading and tennis hardly register as blips on the radar screen. Yet sometimes it is the small things, like the tiny snowflake that turns into a large snowball, which start the wheels of change turning toward something great.

After the quarterfinals of the 2000 U.S. Open, I found myself in a deep funk. At first I assumed that my reaction was normal. I'm a tennis fanatic, and one of my favorite players, Serena Williams, had lost to a player I also liked at the time, Lindsay Davenport. But the next day, while reading the sports section of *USA Today*, I slipped deeper into my doom and gloom. I discovered that Lindsay and the number-one seed, Martina Hingis, had made a ladies' agreement in which they vowed that Serena and her older sister, Venus, wouldn't meet in a history-making final match. An article a few columns over reported that a disappointed Serena had fled New York on the first plane smoking, leaving Venus to fend for herself. I knew that Serena loved and supported her sister but probably needed a break from the media and the fans. She is, after all, only a teenager.

I know it might sound strange, but this situation brought tears to my eyes. But were my tears really for Venus and Serena (two gifted athletes and role models I've never met), or was I crying for all the little girls and boys who would one day find themselves in places and situations in which a great majority of people didn't feel they belonged? I wanted to call Venus and say, "Hang in there, sweetheart. I'm behind you and so is an entire community of people who admire and love you for what your family has accomplished. You make us proud." Somehow I wanted to let her know that she was loved and cherished.

My thoughts wandered back to a time in my youth when I'd found myself in unfriendly territory, and I tried to remember what had given me the courage to press on. When I was a senior at the University of Arkansas (and about the same age that Venus is now), I was the first African American male cheerleader for the football-crazed Razorbacks. My cheerleading partner was a beautiful and sensitive eighteen-year-old freshman named Dionne. Not only was Dionne the same age that Serena is now, she reminded me of Serena in many ways. Athletically built, with a smile that could make a dark room light up like a Fourth of July celebration, Dionne was a young lady who wore her heart unabashedly on the sleeve of her crimson and white cheerleader uniform.

In the late seventies, aside from the fraternities and sororities, the Razorback cheerleaders were among the last of the lily-white organizations at the university. That Dionne and I had been selected to the cheerleading squad was hailed as a major accomplishment by many people on campus, but to the other ten members of the squad we were about as welcome as a KKK member at the Million Man March. My mother was nervous, but Dionne and I weren't afraid or worried because we had not only the support of our immediate family and friends, but the wider support of the African American community (and many others) on campus.

At the first game of the season, the band ushered the team into a stadium filled with 56,000 screaming fans. I must admit, a little bit of fear crept into my body when the head cheerleader, who had barely said five words to me since the tryouts the previous April, informed me that I would lead the squad onto the field. Were my mother's fears valid? Was there an angry redneck with a high-powered shotgun in the stands waiting for me? My concerns proved to be unwarranted, but still, to this day, I don't know why I was asked to lead the squad on that particular occasion and was never asked again. Maybe the head cheerleader thought that in my excitement or nervousness I would trip over myself and become the laughingstock of the squad.

The first time we traveled out of town, the four white male squad members quickly chose partners to share the king-size beds in the hotel room, leaving the cot for me. I didn't mind because I had grown up sleeping on something similar. The next day, when we arrived at Baylor Stadium in Waco, Texas, the white female cheerleaders showed up in their crimson sweaters and pleated skirts; Dionne, however, had been told to wear her white uniform. As we took our places on the sidelines, I noticed tears rolling down Dionne's face. I pulled her close and whispered, "Don't you cry. When you cry, they win. Don't let them win. Besides, you look beautiful and everyone will assume you're the captain."

I have been and remain a great supporter of my alma mater, but even today, the Razorback cheerleading squad of 1976–77 is a group whose reunion I would never attend. Dionne and I were treated poorly and on many occasions some of the members were downright cruel. Yet we didn't let it bother us because we knew every African American football player and student at the university had our back. At the first pep rally the Black students turned out en masse and made sure Dionne and I got the loudest applause. As we strolled through campus on our way to practice (where we knew the head cheerleader would rather point at us than voice her directions), we would receive words of encouragement from our fellow students. I fondly recall the time one of the star players, whom I admired but had never talked to, approached me after a game and told me how proud he was to see Dionne and me cheering the team on. The support that we received from our African American community let us know that we were making a difference, and it made Dionne and me stronger. We worked harder and became better cheerleaders; we wanted to be worthy of such support.

When Dionne died suddenly, a few years after her graduation, many of those same students and players filled a tiny church in Brinkley, Arkansas, until mourners formed a line a mile long. There were many white faces in the crowd that day, but none from the cheerleader squad.

I'm sure that Venus and Serena know that they have lots of fans, but do they know that millions of people they'll never meet love them? Wouldn't it be great if the Williams sisters could carry that love with them as they enter unfriendly locker rooms and country clubs all over the world? Or use such love to protect themselves from the people conspiring against them? Can the love and support of the Black community give Venus and Serena the energy and grace to tolerate those who refuse to speak to them, make eye contact, or acknowledge them as the marvelous champions that they are?

I wonder about the legions of little girls and boys who want to be like Venus, Serena, Tiger, or Michael Jordan. Do they know that they have a community of people outside their homes who believe in them and *know* they can accomplish anything with hard work? Has anyone told them?

As a people, we've achieved some of our greatest accomplishments when we stood together and offered support to those standing on the front line—when we marched (even if we only marched in place) with Martin, rode the bus with Rosa, and entered Little Rock Central alongside Daisy Bates and the Little Rock Nine. Look what happened when we showed up in Columbia, South Carolina, and a relic of a flag, representing a history we must never relive, came tumbling down. Think of what happened when we turned out in record numbers at voting booths all across the country to help elect President Clinton. A man who doesn't share our skin color but proved each and every day of his eight years in office that he cared about our community. Sometimes family members don't always look like us.

Think of what we could accomplish in the future if that little Black boy in Macon, Georgia, who was just elected student body president, knew that he had the support of the Black community behind him, and that he could eventually become president of the United States. Imagine if the little girl who writes poetry in South Central L.A. knew that there were people cheering her on, that one day her words would be published and recited by people around the world. Think of the students who have C or D averages and could be inspired to do great things if they knew that someone, somewhere, believed in them. Imagine the power that we'd instill in little boys and girls who feel lonely and different, if we just let them know that they're not alone and that others share their feelings. Think of the kind of change that would occur if we went back to the old days when every adult who lived in your neighborhood treated you like you were *their child*, reprimanding you when you did something bad, or patting you on the back when you did something good. We need to return to community parenting.

We are at our best and most powerful when we stand side by side, hold hands, and inform our brothers and sisters—the ones we know well and the ones we've just met, the ones who make us proud and the ones who make us cringe—that they are loved; that each is cherished . . .

Stanley Crouch

Updating Our Battles

In the big arena of ethnic confrontation that we still discuss as "race" when the scientific world tells us that it means nothing, we find ourselves just as frequently thinking about ourselves and about this country in terms that are equally meaningless. Sure, only a fool would not be able to recognize that color and sex and class and religion still intrude themselves into too many areas where they do not belong. Yet there are also so many reinventions of our nation and of attitudes in the Afro-American world that we should, by now, be considering fresh directions and facing the need to discard those tactics that are now hardly more than entertainment disguised as news. All of the noise about flying the Confederate flag in South Carolina was appropriate. Quite appropriate. After all, the Confederate flag is the symbol of an army filled with men willing to die in defense of slavery, which was defended as an institution protected by states' rights. All of the noise about racial profiling and excessive police force is also important, especially when we realize that negative attitudes toward the police within so-called minority communities already beset by crime actually end up working in the favor of criminals and bad cops. The criminals benefit from the community's alienation from the police, which can make it uncooperative, and the bad cops benefit from the fact that other cops embittered or disheartened by the negative feeling from the community might look the other way when excessive force is used.

Yet one needs to think beyond the way in which the Confederate flag issue and racial profiling were approached. Marching and carrying placards as well as singing or chanting rhymed slogans might work for some issues. Beyond those issues such demonstrations fall down into the arena of political theater, protest entertainment, photo opportunities that now have none of the sting they possessed forty years ago. In 1960, the civil rights movement was in full swing and the nation at large had to decide if it was tired of Negro Americans living in parts of the country where constitutional rights did not obtain if you were Black, Brown, Beige, or Bone. Today, however, with score upon score of demonstrations under their television belt, Americans are no longer automatically touched by the programmatic hoopla of protest. They are much more likely to be cynical or bored, since the good, the bad, the priceless, and the worthless ideas about life in this country have all made use of the marching mode and the hopped-up oratory at the conclusion—including the Ku Klux Klan! So we might bring attention to something through the old marching and singing techniques, but the serious work of changing public policy comes from other directions.

While there might be much said in favor of stopping the Confederate flag from flying from poles on government property, and there is surely a problem with the police in certain times and certain places, sustained images of protest get in the way of a fuller recognition of where Afro-Americans are at this time. One of the things that need to be done now is to make it clear that the country has improved in many ways because Black people are now successful and more organically involved in every level of the national tale than ever. This is clear from the athletic fields to the board-rooms to the military to the president's Cabinet to the Supreme Court to the worlds of technology and so on and on. The reason it is so important to make that clear right now—over and over and over—is that there now exists a dangerously large intellectual crisis within Afro-American life that has no precedent and could result in future setbacks of catastrophic proportions. We now have younger Black people, regardless of class, who have been misled into believing high grades, command of the English language, punctuality, being reliable, and setting aside the provincial in the interest of developing sophistication are all signs of "selling out," of "trying to be white."

The most remarkable thing about this nationalism of defiant ignorance is how far removed it is from the Black traditions that held sway at least until the end of the 1960s. Before that time, there were no concessions to an exclusive idea of what are now called "white middle-class values." It was not generally believed that subtle or dramatically complex worlds were innately off-limits to Black people. In fact, there was a very real understanding of how important a high-quality education happened to be. Black people knew that their fates were far more easily handled if they were well educated than if they weren't. It was, therefore, no accident that there were so many Negro colleges started in the wake of the Civil War. It was no accident that slave owners thought it dangerous to allow their chattel to become educated, which Frederick Douglass relates to us when writing of how his mistress was discouraged from teaching Douglass to read by her husband. The master knew that education might incline a slave toward dissatisfaction with his position in the world, might lead him to rebellious thought, could aid him in putting together a strategy for escaping the plantation.

Beyond the plantation and beyond Reconstruction, racist whites waged terrorist campaigns against Black schools, fearing nothing more than educated Negroes. What had been very clear before a bizarre kind of rebellion against what later were called "white middle-class values" came along with many other confusions. What was never in doubt was the realization that education, that learning ability, that visions go beyond the provincial. In a progressively complex world, this kind of thinking is tantamount to career suicide. This Information Age opens up many new frontiers through the Internet, but those who can neither read nor write well are primitives within their own era. As such tragically backward people, they lack the skills necessary to make places for themselves in this era, when there are not only many opportunities outside of the blue-collar arena but many inside it as well. Eighty-dollar-an-hour jobs are available in small factories that are understaffed because so few people know the algebra needed to program the industrial robots.

So I believe that at least part of what is to be done must be a focus on everything within contemporary Negro culture that elevates anti-intellectualism. Studies of Black attitudes toward learning have been telling us of these problems for fifteen years. Tests have made it obvious that the problems have nothing to do with learning capacity. By rejecting supposed "white values" and "white standards" in pursuit of "keeping it real," far too many kids are not asserting the Black tradition of excellence as the antidote to stereotypes and best defense against life's unfairness.

It is especially ironic that this is happening at a time when there is so much clear thinking on these issues. The NAACP, the Urban League, ministers like T. D. Jakes, and organizations such as the Career Communications Group and the National Professionals Network are both urging Black people toward entrepreneurship and helping provide pathways into the contemporary labor world of technology, which stretches from the automobile industry to the designing and the building of the most sophisticated computer machinery. In this new world, competent people of every hue and both sexes are sought by companies struggling to maintain their positions in the business or strengthen the one they already have. There have probably never been more opportunities than there are now. This is definitely not the time to spurn education or to reject sophistication—if there ever was such a time for such foolishness.

So what we need now, as much as anything else, is to reassert those traditional Afro-American standards of shooting for excellence. Everyone from men and women on the street to teachers and members of the civil rights establishment should join in that struggle. It can make the difference between falling behind and moving forward.

Tyra Banks

Getting Along

Love each other
Support each other
Uplift each other
Stop "player hating" each other
Can't we all just—well, you know . . .

Full Political Participation

Many avenues of struggle are necessary for our liberation as a people and to become full citizens of the United States— religious and moral values, education, access to capital and economic development.

None, however, is more important than the full use of our potential political power. President Clinton was nominated in the Democratic primaries in 1992 with about 5.5 million votes. He was elected in 1992 and 1996 with 43 and 47 million votes respectively. In 2000, there are 34 million African Americans—23 million of whom are eligible by age and citizenship to vote. The problem is, only about 15 million of us are registered and just 11.5 million actually voted in these two presidential years— many fewer vote in nonpresidential elections. That means we are using only half (or less) of our potential political power. If we use the rod that God has given us—the vote—He will "make a way out of no way." If we don't, that rod will atrophy, turn into a snake, and go to state legislatures, governors' mansions, Congress, and the White House and bite us with poisonous fangs.

Why politics? Political rights are protective of all other rights. Every right we now have, need, or can hope for—public accommodations, equal opportunity, voting rights, the right to employment making a livable wage, quality health care, affordable housing, a quality public education, a clean environment—all will come through political struggle that, in the end, will be codified in the law through some political institution.

Second, politics is the distribution system for the economic system. It determines who gets what, where, when, why, how much, for how long, and what it is called—welfare or a tax break. There is no such thing as "not being involved in politics." When we are born, the state gives us a birth certificate and when we die, a death certificate. Thus, from womb to tomb—the dash on which we live is political. The issue is not whether you will be politically involved, but whether you will be consciously, intentionally, and knowledgeably involved.

While there is no single answer, for progressives there is one priority and one context in which all the other areas, in fact, do operate, and that one area is politics. For progressives, however, that priority and context must not be just politics, but democratic politics! Both words—"democratic" and "politics"—are important for achieving the goals of jobs, peace, and justice and for building a more perfect Union. Unless our politics are genuinely democratic and participatory in the broadest possible sense, our politics will increasingly become elitist, undemocratic, unrepresentative, dominated by corporate interests, economics, and ideology, which can ultimately become authoritarian.

There is no other single act than full political participation—registering, voting, educating, and involving ourselves in the public policy debates and issues that confront us every day—that would make as much difference in our material lives as politics.

Rebuilding Black America ·

"How do we make Black America better?" I would liken the rebuilding of Black America to that of rebuilding a powerful corporation that has lost its way and is trying to find itself again. They got so busy growing that they forgot who they were. Whenever you try to restructure or rebuild a company or individual trying to make a comeback, the first question to ask is: What was it doing that made it successful in the first place? What things did it believe in? What morals and beliefs were important to it before the success? When a company or individual is struggling, his spirituality is strong, because he needs something to lean on to help make a way out of no way. But when good times start coming, and he achieves a little bit of success, he starts to think that he alone is responsible for his achievements. Humbleness is the first thing to go out the window.

Young people confuse humbleness for weakness. Being humble is not the opposite of being confident. The truth of the matter is that humbleness comes from having the utmost confidence, but a confidence that comes from knowing that you did not do this by yourself. All successful people are an amalgamation of all the people who helped them along the way. No man/woman is an island and no one can make it by himself or herself. So we help one another and acknowledge that help to make it back to the top.

EDUCATION: When did it become popular in the Black community to be dumb? Why is it that the child who works hard in school is taunted by his peers and is told that he/she is not Black because he/she spends his/her time trying to improve himself/herself scholastically? Thug life is honored and worn as a badge of courage, as if that is the definitive true Black person. HAVE WE LOST OUR MINDS?

When I was in high school, I rented a film from the library (I guess I am lucky I did not get jacked up for "trying to be white" and going to the library), *Black History . . . Lost, Stolen, or Strayed*. It was narrated by Dr. Bill Cosby. The film dealt with all the "real" history of our people, the things that never made it to history books. Things like our history with math (oh yeah, baby, we were bad with some math), the inventions that we created, in other words . . . THE TRUTH! I sat there with my mouth open, thinking that I would have to search out our true history so that I might know who I am. And to this day I am still searching, putting things together piece by piece. History . . . we have to know from where we come. We have to crave knowledge about ourselves. It should be a never-ending search with our people to constantly seek out the truth about ourselves. Then we must pass that truth on to the generations that follow us. That means you must care about things that are greater than just your individual person. Black people cannot afford to be selfish. It just doesn't work for us. It never has and never will, so quit tripping on life being harder for us . . . yes, it is! So the question is:

What are you going to do about it? Just whine and quit, OR step up to the plate like ALL the generations before you and BEAT them! It is totally up to you.

RESPECT: We must start respecting one another's differences. There is no one definition of a Black person. We are so diverse as a race, which is what makes us so special. So quit being the "keeper of the Blackness" and deciding who is Black or what behavior is Black. Work on your own Blackness . . . that should keep you plenty busy enough. We must respect our elders, for they are you. There is a recent trend to disrespect elders in our community. There is no faster way for a culture or society to fall than to disrespect the elders. We have to train the young ones . . . four to eight years old . . . so that all hope is not lost.

COMMUNITY: How do we get back on track? The old school way. IT TAKES A VILLAGE TO RAISE A CHILD. We must start taking care of the whole community, not just the ones that belong to you. Mentoring, sharing, fostering, adopting . . . whatever it takes. We cannot count on others to help us. That doesn't mean we don't hold them accountable, just that we must take care of ourselves. We cannot just complain about our schools, we must go into them and fix them. Volunteer to work in some capacity at your children's schools, or if you don't have children, just pick a school and help out. If you don't have time to be there physically, then donate something: computers, tutoring time (pay for someone else to help), books, etc. We have the resources to consume everybody else's stuff, let's start giving back to us for a change.

We are faced with a challenge . . . ARE WE GOING TO SURVIVE AS A PEOPLE INTO THE NEW MILLENNIUM? I am optimistic, that is the way my parents raised me. I believe we have one more chance to fix this. But if we miss this opportunity, then as Dr. Martin Luther King, Jr., said . . . "WE SHALL PERISH AS FOOLS."

Leveraging Our Power

Though I contributed to its funding, business kept me from attending the historic and compelling Million Man March in Washington, D.C., a few years back. Two of my sons, Johnny and Michael, did go, and they were as moved by the experience of being there as I was watching it from afar. The television and newspaper images of one million Black men, well disciplined, organized, and happy, as well as proud to be with each other, resonates in my mind still.

There were many political and social factors involved in the march, but to me the most important aspect was the symbolism of these Black men coming together in a show of solidarity and strength. That made me proud, and it gave me hope for our future.

The march emphasized one of the primary messages I try to convey both in *Black Enterprise* and in my personal travels around the country: Our only hope as African Americans in this hostile world is to march, work, and strive *together*. But even that will not be enough for true and lasting improvement. We must learn to *leverage* each gain as it comes, placing particular emphasis on the economic conditions in our community. If we don't leverage our collective economic, political, spiritual, and cultural power, we can never expect to control our own destiny in this country.

We have to leverage our strengths to force open closed doors, whether those doors lead to union jobs, corporate positions, gated communities, or private schools. We have to form a united front of all Black men, women, and children and work toward true equality—economic equality. We have to force the world to understand our value and our significance in every aspect of society, but particularly in the world of commerce.

We must make a renewed commitment to Black consumer activism to demand the respect that our buying power deserves. Before we buy their products, we need to ask Microsoft, Intel, Sony, Polo by Ralph Lauren, and Lexus (just to name a few) to prove that they understand the true economic value of the African American market.

When their responses are unsatisfactory, we need to challenge them. E-mail them. Write them. Telephone them and any other company that grabs your dollars without acknowledging your importance. If we did this often and consistently, we could force their hands. If we pulled together to support each other publicly every time one of us ran up against racism or the iron ceiling, we could change things.

We have not done this enough in recent years. Perhaps we have been too distracted by our individual struggles, but we need to restore communal spirit and bring discipline to our dealings with those who threaten our progress and our economic viability. Everywhere I turn these days, it seems we have given up too much ground.

We cannot afford to take the attitude "I've got mine and I'm not rocking the boat." Too often we are shortsighted, expecting an immediate return, when we should act with the long-term benefits of the greater community in mind. What sense does it make to send your sons and daughters to the finest schools for the best degrees if they cannot graduate and enter the market at a level befitting their training and knowledge?

In the 1960s, when Black ministers carried the cross of leadership for civil rights and the elimination of Jim Crow, we came together behind them. In the 1970s, when Black community activists led demonstrations and marches for better jobs, housing, and education for African Americans, we marched with them. In the 1980s, when Black elected officials were swept into the U.S. Congress, state capitols, and city halls across the nations, giving a generation of African Americans its first real taste of political power, we voted for and supported them. With the business, economic, and employment gains of the late 1990s, many of us were able to move forward a step or more on the success ladder, but too many more of us continued to tread water or, worse, fell even further behind.

In this new millennium, we must come together again to defend and protect the gains we have made and to make sure that we *all* continue to move forward. At the heart of every battle we've faced was the fight for economic equality, the right to compete and have equal access to the opportunities that remain this nation's great promise. African Americans have the same rights to these as other Americans, but we have not leveraged our power as the Jewish people, the Irish, the Asians, and others have—by tapping into the *collective* strength of our businesses and financial powers.

While most of our time is spent—as it should be—in making certain that the bottom line is taken care of, we also need to be watchful of what government is doing, not just to our business opportunities but to the viability of African Americans in this nation. As with big corporations, we need to let the politicians know we are watchful. We must make our voices heard and our weight felt, and we must *never* give our support simply because we have traditionally given it. It has to be earned.

Now more than at any time, African Americans have the leadership and collective wealth that if properly leveraged can give us the clout to attack racism on all fronts. Meanwhile, racism is more insidious than ever, and we have not truly come together, as we have in the past, to fight it.

The success of Black-owned businesses demonstrates the continuing vitality of the American dream. Through the development and growth of such businesses, societal disparities in income and wealth are narrowed, hopes for individual achievement are realized, and national purpose is reaffirmed. It's time we got angry and leveraged our clout. It's time we stopped making excuses. In the past we have expected others to do the lobbying for us, but we can't do that now. We must do it ourselves, for ourselves.

Hardly a day goes by that I don't hear some Black person somewhere ask: Where is the next Martin Luther King, Jr.? Where are our leaders of the future?

While it would help to buoy spirits and direct our efforts if there were one or two breakout personalities we could rally behind, the fact may also be that we don't need another Martin Luther King, Jr. The nature of our struggle has changed. It is clear today—as it has been for several years—that there will be no further interest in our demand for moral justice until we command the significance that only economic power can engender. It is also clear that we must stop looking outside of ourselves—individually and collectively—for the leadership that will create that economic shift. Nobody's going to do it for us. We need to practice leadership on a daily basis as individuals. We need teachers, doctors, ministers, fund-raisers, business owners, and workers everywhere to practice leadership by acting for the good of their fellow African Americans wherever necessary.

How does that translate into your day-to-day reality? The answers are really quite simple. If you are in a position to hire or promote people, look out for your own. Help them get where they deserve to be. That's leadership. If you are a minister, preach self-preservation and self-determination rather than simply exhorting the faithful to count on personal salvation in the next life. That's leadership. If you are a teacher, reach out to your troubled Black students, don't shirk from them in fear and disgust. That's leadership. If you are a parent—a mother or a father—*be the absolute best parent that you can be*. That's leadership, possibly at its purest and most powerful.

If you are on the board of directors of a company that isn't doing all it can to hire and promote African Americans, stand up and tell the board what they need to do. If necessary, show them how to do it. Inform them that it makes good business sense to hire us, not because it's the right thing to do from a social perspective, but because it's the right thing to do from a *business* perspective. Just as our creativity has brought broader expression into music, filmmaking, and all of the arts, and as our athleticism has pushed the envelope in sports worldwide, so have our contributions in business brought fresh ideas and a greater vision to companies in the United States and throughout the world. Drive that point home. Use your perspective, your experience, your guidance to improve the lives of other Blacks within your sphere of influence. That's leadership.

If more of us lived our lives like that, no one would have to ask where our leaders of the future were going to come from. If more of us lived like that, the battle for economic parity along racial lines would be far closer to its conclusion. If more of us lived like that, not only would Black America be better, all America would be better.

Behaving Better

O ne of the things that must happen in our community, as we advance into a new century and especially a new millennium, is a renewed commitment . . . a commitment to our families, others, and ourselves. A commitment to promote those ideas and values that take us back. Back to the time and place where we believed that we were the keepers of our brothers' history. We must believe that the investments we make into our community today will yield successful returns for those who come after us.

There is no magical formula to making Black America better. In order for us to be better, we must act better. Better toward our families, others, and ourselves.

Chuck D

A Community of Accomplishment

There are still major factors that continue to keep America rusted at the root. A public consensus remains that actions speak louder than words; however, apologetic words are a lot better than silence. The silence of Uncle Sam has been mistaken, by some, as good old American racism. In other words, silence has been a contribution to the pattern of the past. Bill Clinton at least started the ball rolling by apologizing to Black folks for U.S. slavery.

Okay, cool. But what must then happen is action after the words, of course. To fix America is akin to fixing a car with many problems. You don't just shine it, change the wheels, and call it a done deal. You have to get under the hood.

Control of education, economics, and enforcement is still a fantasy to the descendants of slaves in the United States. Those three factors are key in determining whether an environment is a community or a plantation/ghetto. Reparations will continue to be a touchy issue for non-Blacks who maintain that they weren't there in the beginning without realizing that they've benefited at others' expense.

Education

America should and could consist of a worldly people who recognize who they are and from where they came. Yet people need the proper preparation to understand and control their own destiny. Americans continue to believe that our 2,000-by-3,000-mile area is the be-all, end-all of the world (save a few jet-set trips to Europe) and slap derogatory labels on other countries like "Third World" (completely skipping over the Second World). Our contributions to the planet are ultimately capsized by our immense ill will. With education, people could gain a broad perspective, unlimited in the knowledge of different lands and cultures and in understanding. But by propagandizing people in the education system, you end up with a processed people, not unlike the processed chickens and cows being injected with hormones. We're shot up with American homogeneity.

The educational process is one-sided. Even though people say supplemental education should come from the home, slavery was such a traumatic experience for so long a time that the paradigm is highly unbreakable without a countertraumatic program. People need to learn what this country did to become the mighty United States of America. It wasn't all so peachy keen.

Economics

Education should teach people to have and support their own. The whole situation of supercorporations eating up smaller entities takes advantage of the community as it loosens people's sense of togetherness. For example, the Black community has never been tight because it is still suffering the posttraumatic effect. The reliance on the supercorporation is a relationship similar to that of the slave to the master owner for necessities and existence.

And what about supercorporations' investments in prisons? That's legalized slavery for the twenty-first century. If you don't have a system that lays out options and education, the people who are suffering the posttraumatic effects of slavery will be conditioned to go right into jail: from one big institution that doesn't supply you with the goods to another.

Supercorporations

Supercorporations influence the "dumbing down" of Americans. If they foster Americans' cluelessness by not recognizing the rest of the world, then they can program people into being mindless drones. When people don't have control over their realities in their communities, a fantasy world (perfect for the consumer) can be sold to them. Americans think they are making the choices for themselves, but they're really just handed down in a candy-coated package.

And the emphasis on athletes and entertainers in the Black community is completely out of hand. It's not *sexy* enough for supercorporations to support scientists or teachers, and therefore they're overlooked when it comes to the big bucks. It all boils down to this: A community that is not given the understanding of its reality will therefore be subjugated to be a slave to a fantasy world. And sports and entertainment are fantasy. Of course, people need releases, but when their outlets become their dependencies, then they're not dealing with the cause at hand. People should be taught to pick and choose their fantasy worlds, not have them forced down their throats.

Ultimately, America needs a sense of worldly accomplishment (look at Thomas Edison, Jonas Salk, and Noam Chomsky or their terribly underacknowledged African American counterparts like chemical engineer Dr. Yvonne Clark, pioneer of blood transfusion science Dr. Charles Drew, astronaut Guion Bluford, and newspaperwoman Pearl Stuart) to advance human beings forward to a point where we can take care of the world and make it a wonderful place to exist all the way around, not just in different pockets.

The Digital Age

I founded my company, DME Interactive Holdings, Inc., in 1994 with the mission of expanding the hardware and software infrastructure within minority communities. After working in the cable industry for a year and seeing the disparities that existed between new digital technologies that were being marketed in 1993 and 1994 in African American communities and Hispanic communities versus majority communities, I decided to do something about it. I quit my job the day after I was married and founded our company in a one-bedroom apartment. Last year we became, after self-financing for the first four and a half years, the first African American Internet company to be publicly traded in U.S. history. Our company is a testament to one thing, and that is that hard work and striving in any community can lead to success.

I believe a strong infrastructure built on education, technology, skills, job development, and placement will strengthen our communities across the country. It is vital that we have skills and tools in the community to participate in the digital world. The digital divide that currently exists is a crisis of such severity in this rapidly evolving digital economy that it threatens to tear at the heart and soul of our progress.

We have created a comprehensive framework through our company, Places of Color, *www.placesofcolor.com,* that provides a wide array of options for African Americans, Hispanics, and other consumers and businesses to get connected, and leads them to culturally appropriate and significant content once online. Our company strategy is to provide each and every family, individual, and business with a computer and the capability to connect to the Internet.

Today, an estimated 65 percent of African American and Latino-American households currently do not own PCs and are not connected to the Internet. In an age when the purchasing power of technology is growing exponentially, we have to rise from being left behind. This will create a solution to bridge the digital divide and build a strong technology-based infrastructure in our communities.

Marian Wright Edelman

What We Can Do

Of course, we can all begin by acknowledging there is much about Black America that has always been good, and there are also many things that have already gotten better. The civil rights movement immeasurably lightened the physical, mental, and emotional burden of growing up Black in America. Millions of Black and poor children of all races have moved into the American mainstream and are better off materially. But something important has been lost as we have thrown away or traded so much of our Black spiritual heritage for a false sense of economic security and inclusion.

We are at risk of letting our children drown in the bathwater of American materialism, greed, and violence. We must regain our spiritual bearings and roots and help America recover hers before millions more children—Black, Brown, and white, poor, middle-class, and rich—self-destruct or grow up thinking life is about acquiring rather than sharing, selfishness rather than sacrifice, and material rather than spiritual wealth. And even as so much progress has been made, for too many Black children and families, progress is not coming quickly enough or at all.

Consider these recent statistics about Black children living in the United States: Every five seconds during the schoolday, a

Black public school student is suspended, and every forty-six seconds during the schoolday, a Black high school student drops out. Every minute, a Black child is arrested and a Black baby is born to an unmarried mother. Every three minutes, a Black child is born into poverty. Every hour, a Black baby dies. Every four hours, a Black child or youth under twenty dies from an accident, and every five hours, one is a homicide victim. And every day, a Black young person under twenty-five dies from HIV infection and a Black child or youth under twenty commits suicide.

The Children's Defense Fund has been hearing many echoes of our trademarked mission Leave No Child Behind® recently; many voices are insisting they too want to leave no child behind. But the reality is that in this time of unprecedented wealth and opportunity in our country, millions of children are still being left behind every day. At the beginning of a new millennium, just as in every other period of American history, many of the children being left behind are Black and Brown.

What can we do? We must begin by insisting that the promise to leave no child behind in our country really means something, and we must hold everyone who makes this promise accountable. In the Black community, we must learn to reweave the rich fabric of community for our children and to reinstill the values and sense of purpose our elders and mentors have always embraced. We must be determined not to let outside forces that have contributed so much to our child and family crises and to making violence ubiquitous in our culture drive or shape our priorities and our values and our children's values. These crises developed over many decades and will not be solved overnight or without a fundamental transformation of our personal, community, private sector, and public values and priorities. But we have transformed those values and priorities in our country before, and it is time to do it again.

Our community richly embraces the legacy of the civil rights movement and we have already reached a point where many people look back at that time with a sense of reverence, as if those heroes and heroines and their brave actions cannot come again. But as extraordinary and singular as many of the individuals in that movement were, the civil rights movement was driven by the thousands of extraordinary and yet ordinary men, women, and children who simply decided it was time to do what they could to stand up against injustice. That time is here again, and now we must pick up that movement's unfinished work on behalf of our children. Mrs. Rosa Parks said on the first Stand for Children Day in 1996 that "if I could sit down for freedom, you can stand up for children."

And stand up tall and together for children we must. A massive new movement must well up from every nook, cranny, and place in our community involving millions of parents; religious, civic, educational, business, and political leaders; and youths themselves. This movement must insist on treating all children fairly and making sure every child receives a Healthy Start, a Head Start, a Fair Start, a Safe Start, and a Moral Start in life and successful passage to adulthood with the help of caring families and communities. That is CDF's goal and that of the Black Community Crusade for Children (BCCC), which is dedicated to really making sure no child is left behind. This will be difficult, but like so many other difficult tasks worth doing, it is possible and necessary. This new movement will answer the question of what we as a community and we as Americans really value and believe in as a people. It will make Black America better, and save America's soul and future. After all, children are our future and every child is a sacred gift of a loving God. If the Black community and nation cannot agree on anything else, we must agree on saving our children right now—all of them.

Farai Chideya

Try, Try, Try . . . to Teach All Children Well

During the 2000 Republican Convention, I went a few miles down the road from the politicking and watched rows of young Black girls sway and sing a song. The lyrics told them that all they had to do to succeed was "Try, try, try/try and try again." The words had substance for them—at least I hoped they did—because they came from an inspirational song by Jill Scott, a breakthrough recording artist from their own struggling North Philly neighborhood.

If there's anything that will allow us African Americans to surmount the challenges that face us—and to derive enjoyment from the world around us—it's education. So when I spoke to these smart North Philly kids about success and careers, I tried to tell them the same thing the song did. I told them that even though most of them had already seen bad things happen to good people, even to themselves; that even though they might have to learn from worn-out books sometimes, their dedication to knowledge would stand them in good stead.

As part of the Inner City Games program, run locally by Donna Frisby-Greenwood (who also helps champion Black Youth Vote), and nationally by Arnold Schwarzenegger, these students worked on sharpening their academic and physical skills over the summer. Most of their classmates hadn't had the opportunity, just one of many reasons test scores in neighborhoods like North Philly remain low.

It's easy to try to get political mileage out of America's education woes. George W. Bush has called the gap between haves and have-nots an "education recession," and blamed it, predictably, on the Democrats. In truth, there's enough blame to go around. The Clinton Administration has provided additional funding for Head Start, early reading programs, and higher education initiatives like the Hope Scholarships. But the problems of American education are so deep that even good programs such as these are like spot treatments on a carpet in need of a deep shampooing. It's not time to throw the rug out (as proponents of voucher programs suggest). It is time to make sure we truly overhaul the system.

For Black Americans, educational inequality isn't just about racial inequality, even though white parents (especially in the South) have a poor record of funding majority-Black school systems. One of the most basic issues is wealth and poverty. In this country, according to a source no less respected than the Federal Reserve, the rich really have been getting richer and the poor have been getting poorer. It's hard for children to learn when they're hungry (one-third of children experience hunger each year) and when their parents are stressed and worried about money. Raising the minimum wage and moving toward a living wage will begin to provide basic support for lower-income families.

In America, unlike many other nations, school funding is linked directly to local property taxes. As long as that is the case, schools in poorer neighborhoods will lack the resources of better-off districts. The Council of Great City Schools estimates that urban schools are underfunded by $3 billion, compared to their suburban counterparts.

Of course, money isn't everything. Teachers unions, despite their generally good intentions, will have to relax their grip enough to let go of the underperforming classroom teachers who turn off the lightbulbs in children's heads and drive principals mad. The charter school movement can help bring principals into the system who will craft independent-minded public schools tailored to the needs of their students, while programs like Teach for America are helping to recruit and train dedicated nontraditional teachers. And despite the long distances children sometimes travel to go to school, parents still have to remain involved. Congresswoman Eleanor Holmes Norton of the District of Columbia notes that the most successful schools in her District, regardless of race or income, have high parent involvement.

When my grandmother went to high school, education was an entirely different affair. The yearbook, for which she was the poetry editor, is filled with pictures of sleek, serious-looking young men and women whose studies probably equaled a college education today. They were the pride and joy of the community, the "talented tenth"—even got to listen to Cab Calloway perform for them. The trade-off, of course, was access. In the 1930s, a huge proportion of students, Black or white, never even graduated from high school.

Today, we are lucky enough to live in a country where most Black students graduate from high school. The quality of their education, however, is far from guaranteed. No one magic-bullet program will end the "education recession." But for the sake of all children, we have a clear mandate: "Try, try, try/try and try again."

Bishop Noel Jones

Change the Children

So proficient at being deficient
No discerning only learning not to care
    for knowledge.
Party hearty, wag your tail, ignore your head
Can you stay a commuter to buy a computer?
A car is more impressive
Hello ignorance, so regressive
Hello illiteracy, so oppressive.
Please number-one consumer
    come home with a computer
And change the children.

Seeking solace outside the pad
    torn to shreds
In absent fathers we dread
With no one around to pass as head
Now there is "no place like home."
    So to the gangs we go
        Totally "gun" ho
        Death without murder raps to shun

The Ku Klux Klan never had such fun
than watch us doing it to ourselves.
So before we genocide on self-inflicted crime
    Daddy please come home in time
To change the children.

So in and out of jail
Learning to read; sad it is only mail.
But in the wrong places
Just food to an inglorious system
    that swallows coloured faces
Let's focus on the injustice of justice
    that epitomizes "Just us."
Set to crucify without thought to correct
Designed to break down and not redirect
Somebody please warn the children.

    Our love for music, who can deny
    We are rhythmic to the bone, that's no lie.
But should our proclivity for obscenity
    dull our sense of responsibility.
    How can we insult our Maker
    With demeaning words for the
        feminine gender?
    How can we appreciate what we
        depreciate
    And give value to what we devalue?
    When even Jesus was born of a woman.
    So before we desecrate our origin
Help us change the children.

Sexually permissive doing the prohibitive
    so uninhibited
A heavenly rush to ecstasy of sexuality
But a hellish hush to the horror of
    responsibility.
Abortion to eliminate this pain,
Only leaves us insane.
So we took care of the physical
Then lost the psychological
Pray tell what did we gain, please,
    other than another disease,
So before we infect all our partners
Let's change the children.

    Religious delusion
    Too much confusion
So the ritual goes on and on
    if the truth be told
    who's REAL in the fold?
So the ritual goes on and on

    Righteous Bigotry?
    Conservative sanctimony
Makes Church a house of racial divide
So the ritual goes on and on
    Expecting generosity
    Without liberality
    Enrich the Greedy
To Hell with the Needy
But the ritual goes on and on.

How can we worship THEE above
When we substitute piety for love.
   PLEASE, GOD, CHANGE THE CHILDREN.

Change the children
We've gone wrong too long
  "Save the children"
Remember the song
  Change the children
We lost our way
  Change the children
Please start today.
For the future is awfully insane
  if the attitudes of our day remain
  Change the Children.

Na'im Akbar, Ph.D.

Making Black America Better Through Self-Knowledge

The ultimate effectiveness (power) of any group of people is the degree to which they have an awareness of who they are and respect for themselves. One of the major deficiencies of the African American community is the persistence of a fundamental lack of self awareness and a debilitating deficit of self-esteem. These characteristics are not new for the African American community, but are deeply rooted in a tradition that was devised to sabotage our collective and personal efficacy and make us into a permanent servant class in America. All of those cultural and institutional devices that are usually employed to ensure that people will develop an effective self-awareness were systematically uprooted and/or prohibited. The consequence is that African Americans are badly handicapped in competition with other groups of people who are equipped with these fundamental qualities of self-awareness and self-respect.

Beginning with the slavery system and continuing through the post-slavery practices of oppression and discrimination, African Americans were prohibited from engaging in those activities that would ensure the acquisition of basic self-knowledge. As a group, we were systematically degraded by the broader culture in such a way that self-respect was certainly extremely difficult to develop. The instruments that generally facilitate this development of self-knowledge are education, cultural images, and celebrations that build a shared aesthetic, role models, and the projection of cultural heroes and heroines.

How to make Black Americans better? We must make a priority of developing cultural and educational institutions that are geared toward developing African American self-knowledge. It is important for us to realize that we cannot engage in economic and political cooperation, resolving our wide array of social problems or competing with other cultural groups on the planet for resources, until we have a clear sense of who we are. This self-knowledge that should lead to self-respect and self-determination is a prerequisite for the achievement of those objectives of self-enhancement that all people hold for themselves and their future generations.

Educators with a deliberate agenda of cultivating the self-knowledge of African Americans must concentrate on developing learning centers and materials that further this objective. The poorly supported efforts of many Afrocentric schools represent a pioneering effort in this regard. Unfortunately, these efforts have often been dismissed as reversed segregation or other degrading characterizations that have minimized the significance and the broader objective of such educational efforts. The existing educational curriculum for every learning system in America adopts a Eurocentric perspective that facilitates the self-knowledge of European-American learners. We should not begrudge European-Americans the right to maximize the potential of their children and their communities. Our children should also have exposure to a wide range of information about other cultural groups and their accomplishments. The focus of our educational system should be reflective of ourselves, but not to the exclusion of those marginal or minority members who may be present in the learning environment. When there is a limited number of African American students and/or personnel with the skills to address them that prohibits proper educational instruction, then we must develop alternative educational systems that supplement the dominant one. Because of usual distortions of this objective, it is important to emphasize that this does not represent the need of "dumbing down" the learning process. In fact, because of the peculiarity of the "double consciousness" that results from being African and American, I am suggesting the need of "gearing up" our educational experience. Not only should we master the rudiments of "American" self-knowledge but develop an awareness of our unique experiences that equip us to draw upon our special resources.

The handicap that creates people who participate in the self-destruction of our communities is the deficit in their self-knowledge. It is important to make a conscious and deliberate commitment to ensure that the educational experiences of our people further and enhance our ability to know who we are. We must unapologetically create a learning environment that empowers us to be as effective as other communities in the world. We must get away from the imposed analysis that suggests that such an objective is "anti-anyone" or inflates into fantasy the facts of who we are. This is not simply a crash course in Black history, but it must be an integrated experience that transmits to us a form of thinking that generates a commitment and expectation of excellence in every arena of human endeavor. It simply does for us what every other people's educational system does for them.

In addition to the effective educational system that sets as
one of its priorities the cultivation of self-knowledge, the whole
array of cultural devices for image development and transmission
must foster this process of self-awareness. Certainly, the arts,
the media, and the literature of a people focus on creating ideals
and images that constitute a people's aesthetic and their aspira-
tion. In every arena of human activity we must take on the role
of becoming conscious and deliberate image-makers. Whether
musical artists, playwrights, actors, journalists, scientists, corporate executives, or technology engineers, we must structure our
agenda and activities toward the creation of images that transmit
an enhanced awareness of who we are. We must affirm our cultural identity, lift up values of our collective freedom, and project images of our excellence in all arenas of life. We need
street names, monuments, museums, documentaries, libraries,
archives, genealogical societies, and any other mechanism that
permits us to engage in exploration and discovery of who we are.
We even need fantasy heroes and heroines, cartoons and myths
that transmit an appreciation for our unique human potential.
We cannot overstate how incredibly important are the images of
those on whose shoulders we stand. Every cultural group creates
in huge and captivating form ongoing reminders of those who
personify the best examples of commitment to the collective
good.

We can make Black people better by recognizing the importance of cultivating the knowledge of who we are. Then we must
make a conscious decision to create the mechanisms and institutions that research and transmit this knowledge. This self-
awareness process should be the criterion and the objective of
the expression of our art, the development of our intellects, the

creation of our financial and civic institutions, and even the worship of our God. By developing the same kind of respect and love for ourselves that other people hold for themselves we can diminish the plague of self-destructive behaviors that threaten to complete what the genocidal attempt of African enslavement in America did not accomplish.

Charles J. Ogletree, Jr.

The Challenge of Race and Education

The visionary W. E. B. Du Bois reminded us that the problem of the twentieth century was the color of the color line. As we look at the educational system in America, the problem of the color line continues a century later. This country will soon celebrate the fiftieth anniversary of the landmark unanimous *Brown v. Board of Education* decision by the Supreme Court. In issuing what is perhaps the most significant legal decision of the twentieth century, and certainly the most important civil rights decision, Chief Justice Earl Warren, speaking on behalf of a unanimous court, observed: "In the field of public education the doctrine of separate but equal has no place. Separate educational facilities are inherently unequal."

In attempting to assess the *Brown* decision, we must look back as well as look forward. It is noteworthy that the architect of the *Brown* decision, Charles Hamilton Houston, Jr., is not mentioned in the case. This omission is understandable but regrettable. Houston, by all accounts, was the lawyer principally responsible for charting the political and legal course by which *Brown* finally reached the Supreme Court in 1954.

It was Houston's mission to train a generation of Black lawyers to lead the legal battles to obtain equality of opportunity in the United States. It was at Howard Law School that Houston developed the ideas that became the basis for cases like *Brown*. These ideas led to the identification, as early as the 1930s, of Black parents as plaintiffs in places like South Carolina and Kansas to challenge segregated and unequal educational systems.

Houston's initial position was clear and simple: If you insist on separate institutions based on racial classifications, those separate facilities must receive equal resources. Houston assumed that legislators would soon realize that the cost of segregation was too high and that integration was an acceptable alternative.

There is little doubt that both Houston and Thurgood Marshall would lament the racial and economic inequality in the educational system today. What would surely distress them is the fact that nearly fifty years after *Brown,* the public schools in Topeka—one of the sites of the original lawsuit—are still substantially segregated. Moreover, lawyers are still arguing to persuade judges and legislators to end segregation in public education and to give Black children the opportunity that Houston and Marshall thought so important nearly fifty years ago.

For many who question this country's real commitment to end segregation, the slow process of desegregation in public education is not surprising. One need only point to the critical language in *Brown*, which allows states to desegregate schools "with all deliberate speed." That phrase, more than any, captured the major flaw of *Brown,* as well as the current crisis of a segregated educational system.

Nearly fifty years after *Brown,* the vestiges of segregation are still apparent in many of the schools that were the subject of the lawsuit. Those that were identified as almost exclusively white remain so. Those that had substantially Black populations maintain those numbers as well. "All deliberate speed" has in effect meant no speed at all.

Ironically, one unfortunate consequence of *Brown* is that when the Court decided to desegregate the public schools, many Black schools were closed. As a result, Black teachers, principals, and superintendents found themselves with no jobs, or facing demotions to positions of less stature and less pay. In recent years, the Court has been clear in its view that, although there was no intentional effort on the part of the public school officials to maintain a segregated school system, the effect of the slow process of implementing the principles of *Brown* is that the segregated system continues to exist.

Even more disappointing is the fact that the segregation in public elementary schools is now being played out in many state universities. Following the logic of *Brown*, minority plaintiffs sued Mississippi because state officials had failed to provide equal resources to historically Black colleges. Several years ago, the Supreme Court concluded that in Mississippi, as well as in other states, predominantly white institutions remained so decades after *Brown*, and predominantly Black schools have not changed as well. The Supreme Court ruled that the state must reexamine those policies and take steps to eliminate the segregation of the 1990s.

The time has come to reexamine this incredibly cautious approach to desegregation. Either the states must be compelled to provide equal funding to Black institutions or they have to take meaningful steps to ensure that sufficient resources are provided to support minority students' opportunities to succeed in integrated settings. The time has come to return to the original strategy of Charles Hamilton Houston, not as a surrender to segregation but as a pragmatic means of pushing our country toward the still unfulfilled promise of *Brown*.

Brown was a historic and important step in the right direction to achieve full equality in education. However, given the current status of segregated education, it is clear that as far as we have come, we've got far to go.

Historically Black Colleges and Universities

"Tom Joyner, why do you ONLY raise money for Black kids to go to Historically Black Colleges and Universities?" Whether that question is being asked by Lesley Stahl on 60 Minutes or a Tom Joyner Morning Show listener on "Open Lines Thursday," my answer is the same. "You can't help everyone." I'm the kind of person who likes to focus on one area. Admittedly, I don't know a whole lot about a whole lot of things. But back in the day when I decided to get into radio, I gave it all I had. And thankfully, I've been pretty successful at it. Radio has been very good to me. But before I even recognized my calling in that field, Tuskegee Institute, now known as Tuskegee University, a Historically Black College, nurtured me and others like me who might have been lost in a different kind of learning environment. It surprises me when I meet Black people who say they wished they had been familiar with HBCUs when they made their decision to go to college, because the decision was made for me probably before I was born. My grandparents on both sides, my parents, and my older brother Albert all went to HBCUs. When my sons, Thomas, Jr. (Killer) and Oscar (Thriller), were old enough to think about attending college, I told them they could go anywhere they wanted, as long as it was an HBCU.

I wasn't the best student in the world, but what I did gain from my five years at Tuskegee—yes, I said five years—was a sense of pride in what Black people had done, as well as a heightened level of confidence in what I could achieve in the future. I wish every Black kid could go to an HBCU, but that's a lot to ask for, even for a big dreamer like me.

So a more feasible wish of mine was for the thousands of kids who do apply, get accepted, and attend HBCUs to have the financial resources needed for them to complete their education. And that's the sole purpose of the Tom Joyner Foundation. I mean, let's face it, not going to college at all is one thing, but going to college and having to come back home because you ran out of money is a whole " 'nother" kind of thing. You remember how it was when you went off to school, even if it was just a few miles from the house. Your parents and relatives were so proud, you stood up in church and the whole congregation applauded. No sooner had you packed your bags than your dad was already planning to turn your bedroom into that den he never had. And some of you know what it was like when the school informed you that you wouldn't be able to register for classes for the next semester because you were behind on your tuition payments. I don't think any kid should have to go through that kind of hurt and humiliation. And I also believe that once a kid leaves to go to college, his parents shouldn't have to give their bedroom back for at least four years. But more importantly, I believe that if a student has the talent, the drive, and, in some cases, the wardrobe, to attend an HBCU, he or she should never be denied because of lack of funds. But I also realize that HBCUs, like all colleges and universities, need money in order to exist and someone has to foot those tuition bills, even if the students and their families can't.

The Tom Joyner Foundation, formed in March of 1998, so far has raised close to $3.5 million and every dime of it has gone to

HBCUs solely for the purpose of helping kids who have run out of money. But along with raising a lot of money for students attending HBCUs, the Foundation has helped raise the awareness of these institutions. Howard, Morehouse, Spelman, and Hampton are Black colleges and universities that most people have heard of, but how about Fayetteville, Paul Quinn, Johnson C. Smith, or Benedict? For a full month these schools and many more (and at some point every HBCU) were spotlighted on *The Tom Joyner Morning Show,* which is heard in more than 100 cities by 7 million people who are mainly African Americans. The presidents of the colleges are invited to come on the air to tout the good things their college or university has to offer, and in most cases, our crew travels to a venue near the campus for a live broadcast that includes a performance from a musical group such as the Gap Band, the Temptations, Morris Day and the Time, and so on. Thousands of dollars are collected at each of these broadcasts from corporate sponsors, alumni, and just plain ol' Black folks who want to help. If you ever had it in your mind that Black people don't donate to anything other than their churches, what I'm about to tell you should change your mind. Most of the money raised by the Tom Joyner Foundation has come from individual donations. During the year 2000, we sent out 15,000 tax-exempt forms to individuals . . . that means that 15,000 Black folks dug deep into their shallow pockets and pulled out money to donate to an HBCU. We've gotten checks from individuals for amounts as small as $9 and as large as $100,000 from an elderly man from Mississippi who donated his insurance annuity to Alcorn. We don't know how happy his grandchildren were about that donation, but we were ecstatic. And of all the thousands of checks we've received over the last three years, almost all of them have cleared! Even the checks we received from my cohost, comedian J. Anthony Brown . . . although his were postdated!

Black kids getting money needed to remain in HBCUs, heightened awareness of HBCUs, Black people coming together to raise money for a common cause, corporate sponsors getting involved—are all reasons to celebrate, and I couldn't be more proud of what the Tom Joyner Foundation has done up to this point. But I would be kidding myself if I didn't face the fact that the future of HBCUs, like so many things we as Black people once took for granted, is shaky.

On the whole, enrollment is down. It's costing more and more to keep the doors open, not to mention the costs of competing with mainstream institutions. And in many cases, the mainstream colleges and universities are more interested in what Black kids can do for the future of their athletic departments than what they can do for our kids' academic future.

Since 1976, at least ten Black colleges closed for lack of funding. In the 1990s three more schools were on the verge of shutting their doors. Our government is withholding funds from some HBCUs on the basis that these Black institutions are discriminating against white students wishing to attend. This really brings things full circle. HBCUs, of course, were created because most white institutions made it impossible for Blacks to be admitted.

If more states follow the lead of California, where race can no longer be factored in for admission to publicly funded universities like UCLA, while at the same time HBCUs are being forced to close their doors, what options will Black kids seeking a higher education have?

I'm just a DJ and I don't claim to have all the answers, but I do hold four honorary doctorate degrees, all from HBCUs, so I have the power to write doctor's excuses for our listeners who want to miss a day of work to attend our live broadcasts. But I also have some suggestions on how we might be able to breathe new life into HBCUs. I've broken it down into three points: consolidate, communicate, and contribute.

I'll begin with the least popular point first. Consolidate. Consolidating with a mainstream college or university is not ideal, but if the alternative is closing the doors of an HBCU, then I think consolidation has to be considered the lesser of two evils. A few years ago, Tennessee State University's state funding was threatened because of a lawsuit claiming it discriminated against white students. Against the wishes of most students and alumni, the HBCU merged with the University of Tennessee at Nashville, actively recruited white students, and continued to receive the aid it needed in order to exist. Tennessee State gave up a lot, but today it's still a thriving institution, while nearby HBCUs Meharry and Fisk struggle to stay alive. I'm not saying consolidation is the way to go, I'm just saying it is an alternative that should be considered.

My second point is to communicate. Those of us who attended HBCUs ought to be singing their praises wherever we go. We need to be out there talking to youth groups, speaking at high schools and trade schools, and communicating the benefits of attending an HBCU. Dig out that FAMU sweatshirt and wear it whether it still covers that belly or not. Be loud and proud of your alma mater.

And finally, my third point is contribute. It's very obvious that HBCUs are in need of money and if you're an alumnus or someone who just cares about the future of HBCUs, your financial support is desperately needed. But just as important as your money is the contribution of your time and talent. Tutor, mentor, volunteer your services wherever they're needed. Come back and work at your alma mater. Become a professor, a coach, a cafeteria worker, a gardener, whatever you can do to make that institution better.

Intellects like to sit around and discuss whether the need for Black colleges still exists. To that question my response is: "Don't make me cuss." We need HBCUs for the same reason we need Black churches, Black radio stations, Black television networks, and Black beauty supply stores. HBCUs meet our needs because they belong to us. They are a part of us. They are us. And we also need HBCUs because Black students who attend them are more likely to graduate. And graduates of HBCUs are more likely to be recruited and hired by major corporations than those who attend white colleges and universities.

And last, face it, where there's a strong Black college, there's a strong Black community.

HBCUs are like family, and like every family there's a member who can use a little help every now and then. If we don't make a conscientious decision to help HBCUs, someday we'll be talking about them in the past tense like the Black banks and newspapers that our communities once depended on. But there could come a time when there will be no Fisk, no Hampton, no Grambling or Prairieview marching bands, no Bayou Classic . . . no spade players! Hey, I don't even want to imagine a world where Historically Black Colleges and Universities don't exist and that's why I'm committed to doing my part toward making sure they're here for as long as Black students are here. But HBCUs have to do more than just exist. The challenge is for us to make them the best they can be so that they can offer the best to our Black youth. What are you going to do to help us meet that challenge? There's an old expression that groups of friends like to use to show their loyalty. "If one goes, we all go." Well, when one HBCU goes by the wayside, in a sense, we all go too. Let's do what we can to uplift the HBCU system and each other.

Dennis Kimbro

Just for Today . . .

It's been said by someone wiser than me that time is money. As we approach the new millennium, that proverb understates the case. Time is a great deal more than money—it's the chance to look back and see what we have done; and to look forward and see what we ought to be. Though we might possess the wealth of royalty when our time comes, we will be unable to buy a single minute more of this precious resource. A minute is a fleeting moment when traveling through the sands of time. But even one minute offers each of us the chance of a lifetime. One minute is ample time to forgive those who have wronged you; long enough to share your heart with those who matter most; plenty enough time to make a difference; and more than enough time to lend a helping hand.

Time is too fast for those who rejoice; too slow for those who feel cheated; too short for those in love; too long for those in pain; and too late for those who feel hopeless. Time is on your side if you use it wisely. Never treat it as if you had an unlimited supply. Here's my advice: In this world, there is no such thing as before or after, on time or late. There is only the peace and serenity of *now*—the now that was, is, and will be. So promise me . . .

Just for today, appreciate the next twenty-four hours and try not to tackle all of your problems at once. Just for today, make this day better than all others. Walk tall and smile more. Don't be afraid to say, "I love you." Don't make the mistake of allowing yesterday to use up too much of today. Just for today, uplift your mind and learn something useful. Read something that is thought-provoking and will improve your outlook. Just for today, find fault with no one. Look for the best in everyone who crosses your path. Give a compliment. It could provide someone with a badly needed lift. Just for today, apologize when you are wrong. Just for today, take the high road. Do the right thing. Just for today, take a risk. You can grow—right here, right now. Embrace every opportunity that may provide a better life for you and your family. Your reward will come if you step out and have faith. Just for today, contact an old neglected friend. Release ill feelings. Let go of an old grudge. Just for today, vow to do something that you always wanted to do. Just for today, encourage a child to do his or her best. Our youth need sturdy shoulders to lean on more than they need critics. Just for today, take care of yourself. Remember, you're all you've got. Finally, just for today, thank the Lord for the gift of life. Let this day be a reflection of the strength that resides within you; of the courage that lights your path; of the wisdom that guides your steps; and of the serenity that will be yours when this day has passed.

Synthia Saint James

Our Golden Age

In Webster's Dictionary of the English Language, Unabridged, the third definition for "millennium" is: "any period of great happiness, peace, prosperity, etc.; an imagined golden age." I've chosen this definition, eliminating "imagined," for all Black Americans, as the basis for our affirmations as we enter into our "Golden Age."

1. Let us, as a people, share great happiness that we are still among the living and therefore can still make a difference in our lives and in the lives of multitudes.

2. Let us strive for peace in our homes, in our communities, and throughout all our worlds.

3. Let us accept prosperity as an innate part of our existence, both human and spiritual, realize it as a blessing given and to be always shared.

4. Let us always remember to smile, our golden smiles, especially when we see and greet each other.

The ability to smile has great powers, affecting all around us. Our smiles have the ability to heal, to give others strength, make others smile and feel happy, and even bring about peace.

Look into your mirror now and smile, smile, and SMILE!

Vivica A. Fox

The New Millennium

The structure of Black family life could be improved. Good old-fashioned morals and discipline need to be reinstated in everyday life.

Let's go back to church and fellowship as a family, as did the generations before us. Have more family dinners where you sit and talk and enjoy the company of one another. Where you talk and really hear what the other person is saying. And don't forget to do it over some good old-fashioned SOUL FOOD! Let's teach our children to care for each other, to respect each other, and to most importantly value life—others', as well as their own. Neighbors and other adults need to return to the old days of watching each other's kids—get involved. (You know when you used to get told on.) We need two adult parents (mother and father) to raise a strong family—God decided to make two parents for a reason. Boys need to learn how to be gentlemen from other men—preferably their fathers. Girls need to learn how to be ladies—preferably from their mothers. We're going into a new millennium; let's go there strongly, intelligently, and until forever.

Jesus

What Black America needs is Jesus. It's a beautiful thing for us as a people to find a church, go to it, and pray, but until we proceed to get the church inside of us, we are still lost. That's how our ancestors made it through slavery and all kinds of obstacles and setbacks. If we come to Jesus naked and unashamed, we'll find our way.

Know—Who You Were; Who You Are; Who You Choose to Be

I have been watching it and writing about it for years. Far too many of us fail to take the time to ask ourselves three very important questions: Who was I? Who am I? Who do I choose to be? Without so much as a vague answer, a hint about your involuntary responses to these questions, you cannot move beyond the chaos and confusion of daily survival.

Every now and then, you must look back and remember all you have gone through; all you have been through; and, more important, how *you* assisted *yourself* in getting to where you now find yourself. Asking, *"Who was I?"* gives you a sense of history. Not just your story—but the history of your skills, talents, and abilities. It is this kind of self-reflection that reminds you of all you have or have not accomplished. More important, reflection lets you know why and how you did what you did. Reflection empowers you. A close and careful review of *"from whence you came"* gives you the power to make new choices for yourself and about your life.

Your life speaks to you. It tells the story of your choices, your priorities, and the vision you hold for yourself. It takes a great deal of courage to ask yourself, *"Who am I?"*, relying on the circumstances and conditions of your life to provide the answers. It is also by asking this question that you can determine whether the life you are living is an accurate testimony of yourself. Your life will tell you the absolute truth about you. The issue is, are you willing to hear it?

Holy scripture, respected prophets, and grandmas have been telling us for centuries, "Without vision, people perish." As we move forward into new times and new dimensions of living, we must know where we are going. *"Who do I choose to be?"* is the question you must ask in the development of a vision. The answers to this question will motivate the choices, activities, and alliances you choose. Those things you choose to do or not do; those people you choose to be aligned with or unaligned with must be in keeping with your vision. When they are not, you will find yourself on a chaotic treadmill of nonproductivity, spinning your wheels in the mud, flinging dirt in your own face. You are your own best friend. If you recognize and understand this, it is imperative that you know who you have been and will be hanging out with, lest you perish.

III

Excerpts from Advocacy in the Next Millennium: A Symposium

which took place on Saturday, August 12, 2000, at the Bovard Auditorium, University of Southern California, Los Angeles

Panelists

Panel I

Raymond Brown, *MSNBC Legal Analyst*
Les Brown, *Motivational Speaker, Entrepreneur, and Author*
Rev. Jamal-Harrison Bryant, *Pastor and Founder of the Empowerment Temple A.M.E.*
Farai Chideya, *Journalist and Entrepreneur*
Stanley Crouch, *Columnist, Author, and Playwright*
Dr. Michael Eric Dyson, *Professor and Author*
Danny Glover, *Actor and Activist*
Earvin "Magic" Johnson, *Entrepreneur and NBA Legend*
Dr. Jawanza Kunjufu, *Educator and President of African American Images*
Dr. Julianne Malveaux, *Economist, Columnist, and Author*
Hugh B. Price, *President and CEO of the National Urban League*
Rev. Al Sharpton, *Civil Rights Activist*
Maxine Waters, *U.S. House of Representatives*

Panel II

Charles Ogletree, *Professor, Harvard Law School*
Dr. Na'im Akbar, *Psychologist and Educator*
Danny J. Bakewell, Sr., *Community Activist*
Johnnetta B. Cole, *Educator*
Nikki Giovanni, *Writer*
Lani Guinier, *Professor, Harvard Law School*
Jesse Jackson, Sr., *Civil Rights Activist*
Jesse Jackson, Jr., *U.S. House of Representatives*
Bishop Noel Jones, *Pastor of Greater Bethany Community Church*
Randall Robinson, *Founder of TransAfrica*
Iyanla Vanzant, *Author and Motivational Speaker*
Cornel West, *Professor, Harvard University*
Malik Yoba, *Actor and Activist*

ADVOCACY IN THE NEXT MILLENNIUM:
A Symposium
Morning Session

Attorney Raymond Brown,
  Moderator

Les Brown   Eurvin "Magic" Johnson
Rev. Jamal-Harrison Bryant   Dr. Jawanza Kunjufu
Farai Chideya   Dr. Julianne Malveaux
Stanley Crouch   Hugh B. Price
Dr. Michael Eric Dyson   Rev. Al Sharpton
Danny Glover   Congresswoman Maxine Waters

Raymond Brown: I am really honored to be here with you today because this is a chance for us to have a conversation. And the conversation is going to include some of the finest thinkers and activists in the country. The freedom struggle didn't start today and it's not going to end today. But what we hope we can do is get some real insight, some real windows on where we are, the challenges we face, and where we want to go from here. Now, if you know these folks as I do, you will know that any one of them could stand up for the next three hours, keep us spellbound, and educate us. But those of you who know

math as well as grammar can figure out that that's just not going to work today. And what we've asked them to do then is to
give us something special. Something different. A conversation. As though they had dropped by your house one day or
were talking to you on the steps of the church just outside. A
conversation about what they really think about the problems
that we face and the challenges of overcoming those obstacles. And what I want to do is ask them to focus on them in a
special way. Now, the other night, Iyanla Vanzant [said], "We
have to talk about truth." And so we're going to have a truthful
conversation from some of the people we respect most in the
country. And we want to talk about some of the tough issues
that we don't always discuss: race and gender and age. And
some of the things that divide us, as well as the things that
pull us together. But let me start with the person I think ought
to be the first person we hear from, because we're here on her
turf, because she's taken on some tough issues that very few
public officials in the country were willing to deal with, like
the CIA and drugs, and because she excited me so much during those Impeachment Hearings. Every time she started
rolling, I just wanted her to keep on talking. I hope if they ever
catch me, she's there to stand up for me. But the question I
wanted to ask you has to do with something that we keep
coming back to. It's one of those traps, Congresswoman
Waters. And that is, it's the trap of many folks who think they
ought to vote and participate in the electoral process, but
every four years seem to be faced by a bunch of Republicans
who don't care—although this year in Philadelphia, they put
on a show that made it look like maybe they want us to think
they care—and Democrats who have a way of taking us for
granted. And I thought maybe, given the fact that you are not

just one of the finest leaders in the country but also bring the special perspective of Black women to national Democratic politics, are there some ways in which you are critical of the Democratic Party? Some things we ought to know about them? Some ways we ought to measure their conduct . . . ?

Maxine Waters: Well, I think it's important for me to have a conversation with my party. And I must tell them that yes I am a Democrat and I consider myself a rather loyal Democrat. But they must understand I'm a Black woman and a sister first. And I think I must say to them, "If you don't believe me, I still call my mama 'Ma Dear.' " And I think I must say to them, "You have chosen your vice presidential candidate. You didn't ask me anything. You didn't consult me. You didn't consult my community. We make up the most loyal base of this Democratic Party. And now we're going to demand something from you. This new vice presidential candidate that you've chosen has got to get rid of his position on vouchers and support public education. We're going to demand that this vice presidential candidate supports affirmative action. And we're not going to tolerate any more 'lock 'em up and throw the key away' criminal justice. And so the task for us, while you ask us to be loyal, and to swallow some things we don't like, we're going to ask you to be loyal to us and have this candidate demonstrate what he cares about us and our community by giving in and changing his position on these issues. And we don't intend to have them 'Sista Soulja' us anymore. And if they attempt to do that, we're going to do a Muhammad Ali ropa dope on them!"

R. Brown: Al Sharpton ran one of the most successful primary campaigns for the Senate of the State of New York, especially given the demographics of that state. So let me expand on

Congresswoman Waters's ropa dope. And if I assume that you agree with her, at least to some extent, what does that mean in concrete terms? What's the alternative?

Al Sharpton: First of all, in concrete terms, is that we can engage the political process at different levels. Uh, we can decide if they don't want to speak to our issues, to vote for Congress down and not deal with the top of the ticket. We can decide to make demands in order to deal with the top of the ticket. Martin Luther King, Jr.'s greatest marches were against a Democrat named John Kennedy and Lyndon Johnson. We can not allow them to say to be loyal means that we must be silent about what we believe.

R. Brown: Stanley Crouch is the only man in America with whom I disagree 90 percent of the time and I still love to hear him talk. Stanley, to the extent that there is this trap that we seem to come to every four years, why are we always in this trap, and is there a way out?

Stanley Crouch: Hello. Well, I think there are a number of things that need to be done. I think there needs to be a very large voter registration. And people need to vote, not just register. They need to vote. Now, Black Americans can decide at any election, who goes in the Oval Office. There are enough of us to do that. But what both parties know is that Black people don't register to vote and, by and large, they vote in lower percentages than everybody else. The thing is that if that changes, if Black people with money begin to create lobbies— that is, people who work for your issues all the time. If a thousand guys, a thousand people with money give up $250 every three months, that's $1 million worth of lobbying right there. That's a lot of money. The thing I'm saying is that I think the mechanics of power have never changed. Now you can get up

and you can go, "Whoa, we ain't goin' let you do this no more."
They heard that. They know that song in every key. But the
thing they don't know is what happens if there's a real mobi-
lization in terms of voting, in terms of lobbying, in terms of
keeping the specific issues in place. Just very, very quickly to
close out, Black Americans are as responsible as anybody for
Nelson Mandela getting out of prison in South Africa. Now,
this was done through the movement to, uh, the divestment
movement on the campuses. Black people on newspapers got
the South African story taken from the back of the newspapers to the front of the newspapers. The sanctions were organized and written by the Congressional Black Congress.
When Reagan vetoed those, there was even more mobility.
Finally, there was organization with Danforth and others [and]
his veto was overridden. Now, this was one of the major
events in politics in the last twenty-five years. Most Black
Americans don't even know that. They think Nelson Mandela
flew out of prison on his own. People just like you in this audience helped to do that. And they can have the exact same effect on domestic policy, I would say.

R. Brown: Farai Chideya, you seemed to be shaking your head
no when Stanley was talking about Black folks and voting.

Farai Chideya: Right, well, you know there's one point I want to
make. It is that we do, we can mobilize. The only group of
people who showed a gain in the mid-term elections, which
are the congressional elections, were Black people between
the mid-term elections in 1998—yeah, '98—[where] we
showed a gain. We were the only people who showed a gain.
Why was that? That was because the last mid-term elections
had brought in the Republican avengers. You know, the
Contract on America. And we were the ones who said, "We

can't take this." And so we showed up and voted in 1998 to push them back. And we almost regained the Congress. And this time we might just do it. And so I think that we need to understand that we do have the power to motivate ourselves and vote. And I think that this time around we may actually have the power to regain a Democratic Congress. I think that we sometimes sell ourselves short; even though we sometimes don't vote, we do have the power and we do have a track record. And another thing that this points out is that people generally, I think, are better at voting out of fear. This is not a racial thing, this is just an observation. People vote out of fear more than they vote out of happiness. When people are happy, they sit around on their butts and relax. When people are afraid, they get out and vote. When people are afraid of the Republican Contract on America, they vote. When people are afraid of people taking away their benefits, they vote. When people feel like they've got a chicken in every pot and a check coming every week, they don't vote. And so what are we afraid of right now? I think we need to be very afraid of another Clarence Thomas or two or three coming into the Supreme Court. That, to me, is the big thing we need to be afraid of right now in terms of the current elections. Because if the Republicans get elected, I mean George W., you know he's got his own issues. But if he starts appointing Supreme Court nominees, the ship is sunk. You know what I mean? So this is something we really need to think about. I agree completely with Stanley that we have the ability to push the ball forward on domestic policy and I think that the new Jim Crow, right now, is the prison-industrial complex. The fact that there are 2 million people incarcerated, 6 million people living under supervision, half of them are African Americans.

We have to deal with this now. Right now. And this movement is bubbling up. The no-more-prisons movement is bubbling up and there is a direct correlation between how much is spent on prisons and how much money is not being spent on education. You know, first people said, "Oh, you know those crazy people on the fringes of society, they're just, they must like crime. They must like drugs." But now, all of a sudden, this is making sense. You have Republican lawmakers, people like Tom Campbell, right here in California, making speeches that people are listening to. And so [the prisons movement] is coming into the center and into the mainstream. People who are in our community started the ball rolling. And I think in the next two, three years you are going to see a widespread move to really change the nature of criminal justice in America. And we just need to keep pushing it forward.

R. Brown: Julianne Malveaux, every time I read your work, I keep coming back to a theme about Black folks spending about $500 billion a year. . . . Of those numbers, what's the likelihood in a practical sense that some of that money can be harnessed for political and other kinds of community-related activities? Or is that just a dream because those are big numbers?

Julianne Malveaux: Clearly our community does have, on one hand, a lot of money, but on the other hand, not our share of the money. The other conflict that we have is that in the American consciousness, on the one hand we have a tendency to look at ourselves as individuals. There's a whole growth of Black conservativism about people standing up and saying, "I'm an individual, I'm not just a Black person." Now, I want to say to them, "You're blessed that you're just a Black person. What else would you want to be?" You know the "incognegros" running around are very dangerous. You know the differences between looking at your individual status and your group status. . . . I just want to give a shout out to Magic Johnson here because he's one of the individuals who really does look at community economic development. I think that he is extraordinarily unique as an athlete because he doesn't have to do it, he chose to do it. And I think that that's something very important. And I think that the question that gets raised is how do we lift up, build up, grow up some more Magic Johnsons? How do we get the folks who have the wealth and the wherewithal to decide that we can pool things together? We don't do anything together. We think that the white man's ice is colder. So we hear Stanley Crouch talking about the fact that we could have a PAC [political action committee]. Maxine, how many PACs do we have? One or two? We don't have enough. We have these other folks who have been lobbying 24/7 about. . . . You can purchase a United States senator. They're very expensive, but you can buy one, you can buy you one if you want to. And so the question becomes how we can put our collective forces together. And we have to begin to make that as exciting as some of the other things we do. We have to trickle that down to our young people. So that it's as exciting as the other things we do. And the individual. . . . There's nothing wrong with individualism, but there has to be a collectivism. One of the things that is really frightening right now is that many of us . . . and I would ask for a show of hands, but there are too many of y'all and I can't count that high, but you know when you look at this economy, it's an economy that is generating "prosperity." And there are a lot of people who feel prosperous. So, as Farai said, when people feel good, they don't feel pain. They don't vote. You have too many African American people who think Clinton has been good to them.

No, Clinton has been good to Clinton. He's the president, y'all not. He did not get to our issues until the last year of his eight-year presidency because we spent a full year fooling with his impeachment mess. What does that mean? It means that the unemployment rate overall is 4 percent. But our unemployment rate is 8 percent. It means that we've experienced economic growth of about 7 percent and about 5 percent a year, roughly, for the past six or seven years. But our community owns 1.7 percent of the wealth of the country.

R. Brown: Is it practical to think about harnessing part of that $500 billion a year, or is that just a number?

Malveaux: No, it is very practical to think about us harnessing some part of it. Let's be clear. Part of our income is not disposable income. You have to buy whatever you have to buy. But there's money that we do not have to spend. Why are we funding Nike? Why are we funding these people who do not support us? Why do we . . . ? If we go back to the 1920s, why do we buy where we can't work? I believe in economic boycotts. I would like to have a simple boycott-of-the-month club. Let's just pick, you know, a Fortune 500 company out of the hat and say we're going to boycott them suckers. Why? 'Cause we want to. Because we want people to understand that we have that much economic clout. What if we said we were not going to buy any more Johnnie Walker Red? You can see the head of that liquor company calling Kweisi Mfume and Hugh Price, probably saying, "Hugh, can you get the brothers and sisters to buy just a little more?" What if we decided we wouldn't buy any more ketchup? Pick any product. What if we decided as a matter of course that we wouldn't march, but instead, put a dollar into some kind of a fund? It is very practical, Ray, but what it takes is our collective will and some very foresightful people saying, "It's time to do this." Now, that's what it takes. We can do it. We've done all kinds of things. We got out of slavery. You know. We, you know, we survived Reconstruction. We could, indeed, have our own banks. Why do we have thirty-seven banks for how many million Black people? And why won't we put our money in our Black banks? The question, Ray, is not is it practical, the question to these, I don't know how many people here, is "What would you do with another Black person economically?" Are you willing to step out and say to build a community, I'm gonna do a Magic Johnson? You don't have as much money as he does, but you can do something along those lines that invests in us.

R. Brown: Hypothetically, let's bring in that we raise $100 million over the next year. I mean put it in the bank and said, "We trust you." We want you to be the first to set an agenda. Give us the priority. What would be the three most important areas in which you would focus those resources in terms of the needs of the African American community at large?

Jawanza Kunjufu: We've had this idea for years that if 35 to 40 million of us all gave $1, I'm a little slow on math, but I think that's $40 million. Uh, we have the numbers and even the homeless have $1. But Raymond, the point that you just raised: "Who would we trust to hold that kind of money?" There's this rumor that in terms of our community, I mean how is it that foreigners can come into the African American community and make more money than we can? And the rumor is that Arabs and Asians received a low-interest loan. But as you know, Rev. Sharpton, in New York City, only one-tenth of the Africans come from the Caribbean. But they own one-third of all the businesses. I mean, the government . . . of our businesses, right. And so the banks did not give Jamaicans a low-interest loan. It is called *Ujamaa* (cooperative economics), it's called *Susu*. And it would work like this: We could have 100 of us come in a meeting like this, and the first step is that everybody brings a business plan. We can no longer just talk about the issues, we have to make it into a plan. The second thing is that everybody brings $100. Rule number three is we all agree whoever has the best plan will receive all the money. Now we have to put that in there because there's a rumor that there's some Negroes, Incognegroes, in the audience who, if they did not win, that they would not want to have the money shared. Rule number four, we're going to keep all the money inside the room. Let's say, for example, Dr. Cornel West— and he probably would have the best plan—he may walk out of here with about $50,000 . . . but, Cornel, you have to understand that's our lawyer. Only work with that lawyer. That's our accountant, that's our marketing firm, that's our printer. We're gonna keep all the money inside this room. Now, later on, I'm sure I'll get some time to talk about education, but the real issue is that when chains are taken off the wrists, but placed around the mind, schools teach more than 3-R's. They teach values. They can teach you to value "we" or "I," cooperation or competition. The internal or the external. And so there are very, very few schools in America teaching our children the *Nguzo Saba* (the seven principles of Blackness), teaching our children "Maat," teaching our children an Afro-centric curriculum. And we have to make sure that's done as well. That's the only way we're going to be able to trust each other.

R. Brown: Brother Kunjufu raised a profound issue about trust. And I told you we gotta talk about some things that aren't always comfortable. Thursday night Rev. Bryant was talking about some of the older leaders who have been active in the movement, and I believe he said two things that struck my ear. One was "Pass the torch," and then he said, "???." Now, I understood what that meant, but I wanted to explore that a little further, especially since Brother Kunjufu is raising the question of trust. I mean, it seems to me that some of the people who've been around a long time have some memory and experience that's useful. What is your thought about the nature of passing this torch [of leadership]?

Jamal Bryant: I'm afraid with the antiquated leadership we have, that we have changed from a movement to a museum. That we see some leaders almost as a "Smithsonian." That when we see them, we're reminded of some golden age in the past, [without] relevancy to our present. I think that one of the mistakes we have made is that we have not let our leadership become democratic. Once you're a [designated] leader, you're a leader for life. And so everything that they say, everything that they represent is out of some vacuum in time . . . it has no relevance to where we are. So every time you bring a gathering together, there's some inference to the March on Washington; there's some reference to Selma. But there's no reference to what's going on in Brooklyn, what's going on in Compton. And so, the masses of young people are asking, "What about me?" and no longer see themselves, uh, because *Time* magazine and *Newsweek* have deputized people to be our leaders and [the leaders] no longer speak to where it is that we are.

R. Brown: Julianne, quickly.

Malveaux: I want to make a really brief point. Jamal talked about age in terms of leadership. And I can't let that pass without talking about gender . . . I want to see women at the leadership table as well. And we cannot have leadership unless we have women there.

Hugh Price: One of the major challenges that we face, when you look back at the African American experience in this country, we basically arrived as slaves, we graduated to three-fifths of a person under the Constitution, and the struggle since then has been to make us five-fifths of an American people. And that's been the battle ever since. A whole person legally, a whole person in terms of the social contract and a whole person in terms of the economics. We have moved significantly forward on legal rights, but there are major issues still abroad in our society. We talked about the fact that Jim Crow is still running rampant in the criminal justice system. We have made some progress on the economic front and we have made some progress on the education front. One of the most influential books I've ever read is a book called *Tribes*. And it talks about how various groups that have been put upon and set upon have nonetheless survived and prospered in the face of that. And they do it in the following ways. They do it by being obsessed with education. We, as a people, have got to be sure that every child, every Black child, comes out of school knowing how to read and write and reason and [use the] computer and navigate the Internet. And if we don't do that, that borders on child neglect by us, if we allow that to happen. Successful tribes are obsessed with being on the leading edge of knowledge, not in the caboose. So we've gotta be obsessed with technology and science, and all of that stuff that's driving the economy. And we are not in that game yet to the extent that we have to be. And they're obsessed with creating business. [Successful tribes] don't worry that much about who's in the White House because they don't allow their fate to turn on what happens to happen in the political process. It's very important to be a player, it's very important to have influence, but you can't come unglued if you don't win. You've gotta have a strategy to go forward. So we've gotta create economic institutions. We've gotta create economic institutions that operate in the mainstream as well as in our communities. That's why when we talk about patronizing Black companies, I'm proud to wear a Wittnauer watch. How many folks know Wittnauer is a Black company? So we gotta build economic institutions that generate wealth, that give us the money to create the PACs, to make Spelman become one of the great institutions under Johnnetta Cole's leadership. That was the Cosbys' philanthropy, bred of money, earned through economic institutions that we control. So that's gotta be the baseline agenda, regardless of what's happening in the White House.

R. Brown: And this morning when I gave up in despair on trying to figure out how to guide a conversation with this many dynamic people, I picked up the *[New York] Times* and, lo and behold, the *Times* is writing about reparations. And, what's even more interesting, three times they quote some guy named Dyson. And the last quote is interesting. This is what he says. This ends the article, which is two pages in the *Times*. "I think" . . . Now remember there's been an article that's pro and it's con. Why there should be reparations and why there shouldn't and they come to Professor Dyson. "I think it's part of the social contract of justice in America that if Black people have done what they've done, and been treated the way they've been treated, then they deserve what they deserve. And we can argue about what the desert should look like, but it ain't come yet." What is the likelihood, given the long history of the reparations discussion in America, which started during Reconstruction, what's the likelihood that that's a realistic way of getting hold of resources from the public sphere that Al Sharpton talked about to use in a way that helps Black folks?

Michael Eric Dyson: Well, I think, first of all, we've got to acknowledge that there's a moral impetus and an ethical imperative behind the argument for reparations. The reality is in American society when it comes to talking about compensation for the people who have been the most loyal, the most committed, the most insightful, the most courageous defenders of American democracy, and lived that democracy while America refused to live it itself, walked it from parchment to pavement, then African American people deserve at least the possibility to be logically considered to be the beneficiaries of the very thing they have made possible in American society. The reality is we know we can't work out the specific algebra or the calculus or the mathematics of how you pay people back for what you have done. You can't pay for what Dr. King called the psychological genocide that has been perpetrated against Black people. You can't pay for the psychic wounds that we have endured. You can't pay for the spiritual malaise to which we have been subjected and that we see manifested in our own communities. But what we can do is to first of all acknowledge the fact that something went wrong and by acknowledging that something went wrong, then we can figure out what will happen. And let me say this, this is why we see the moral devastation and the economic deprivation and the economic restructuring going on in American society. It's not simply about whether or not we are bad or good. It's about people having access to economic resources. If we live in a society where we've got sufficient education, where we can overcome the digital divide, where we have political representation, where we have the ability to articulate our claims without always being seen as "those niggers who are complaining about something, bitching and bellyaching and moaning" . . . we'll show that we are not only able participants in the larger pageantry of American citizenship, but we have held that banner high, even when America refused to acknowledge its worst side that we represent.

R. Brown: [You] have talked critically of some in the hip-hop cultures who have not suggested that they have some moral responsibility. And you also talked about athletes and other Black cultural figures who have not adopted moral standards.

Dyson: . . . I love, I love R&B music. I love a lot of what goes on there, but ain't nobody asking Anita Baker why ain't she making a statement about the deconstruction of misery in American society. Nobody's asking Luther, and I love Luther, put him on every night, "Don't you remember I told you . . ." I love Luther, right, but nobody, but hold on, nobody's demanding that he be morally responsible. This is all I'm saying. As many problems as these young people have, when you talk about racial profiling, now it's a problem in the suburbs of Black America where we can't drive our late-model cars, all of a sudden it's a problem. But when Tupac said, "Just the other day, I got lynched by some crooked cops, and to this day them same cops on the beat getting major paid. But when I get my check, they takin' tax out so we payin' the pigs to knock the Blacks out." All I'm arguing for is, at least if we listen to the misery, the hurt, the pain, the suffering, what we will see reflected in them. . . .

Sharpton: I think what Dr. Dyson is saying right, but I think at the same time, we've got to challenge all of this in the context of where we operate. The fact of the matter is, they don't treat Don King or Master P like they do Donald Trump. So just getting rich is not going to solve the problem. That's one. Secondly, these artists can't just rap Black for white record companies. They got to get in the community like Master P and struggle. They're not the heirs to King. They're the heirs to Sammy Davis and Harry Belafonte and Danny Glover, who was in the struggle. A lot of them are not representing the struggle. They're representing Polygram, Sony, and Atlantic Records. And we don't need them to exploit us either, because they haven't put their behind in a movement.

Waters: I'm always amazed when we expect young people to have more wisdom than we had when we were young. While we're talking about young people, young people don't feel protected by us. We've compromised so darn much they have no respect for us. Every time they look at us and they ask us, "Please do something about us being targeted down here in our cities, where we're being picked up when we're out here doing nothing wrong." But when we compare what is going on in our cities with what is going on in Beverly Hills and other places where they have money to pay for fancy lawyers, we are asked to have our rights compromised away in the courtroom. We are told to plea bargain. When we get caught with five grams of crack cocaine, we get five years mandatory minimum sentencing. While 100 times more powder cocaine is a slap on the wrist. You stay in the state system and you don't get locked up in the federal prison. I maintain that young people should not be involved with possession or trafficking in drugs. [But while] they may be stupid at nineteen or twenty years old to do it, they don't deserve to have the rest of their lives compromised away because they made a stupid mistake. Finally, let me just say this. When we get some starch in our back and we stand up and we're prepared to confront the police, [when] we're prepared to confront the political system, and we're prepared to tell corporate America you cannot buy me, young people will respect us.

R. Brown: Magic, part of this discussion is about you in the sense people like yourself who had amazing success in the cultural arena, or in sports or entertainment, have some obligation to give back. And it's apparent where you stand. In terms of professional athletes and entertaining as a group of folks, to what extent have they been socially conscious in the current generation and tried to commit themselves to the benefit of Black people in a larger sense?

Earvin "Magic" Johnson: Well, first of all, we should give back. I mean most of the people out here on this panel, out here in the community, out here, raised me. We should give back because of that. The problem we have is, first of all, we let our agents and managers speak for us. That's number one. Number two, [Black stars] ask us to buy $150 pair of sneakers for our kids, they ask us to buy the jerseys, the uniforms. But then do you ever see them? Are they in our community? See, they forget where they come from. That's, that's the problem. . . . I think I employ about three thousand Black people. Now, hold, hold. I'm not saying that for applause. What I'm trying to get to is, there's probably about five thousand Black athletes, probably in all the sports, I believe. If you take that number of Black athletes, times three thousand, where are we at? A million-five, I think. Employed Black people. We think that we have arrived and made it by going out buying 100 cars, a big gold medallion around our necks, but we have not arrived. Because one thing that we forget, we don't own anything. They're gonna let us play. We have entertained them for years. We are the best at entertainment. But we don't own no teams. We don't own no record companies. No movies. Same situation.

R. Brown: Why is that? Is that solely because of people stopping us, or do we stop ourselves?

Johnson: No. We stop ourselves because what we've been talking about is coming together. You can't get us all in a room to come together for anything. Because our egos get in the way. It just bothers me that we can make $20 million a year, $17 million a year, and yet you guys are responsible for those people making that type of money. . . . I say that because the grandmothers, the uncles, the guy down the street, you looked out for me. You looked out for the guys who have made it in some fashion. But we will not come back in our own community. . . . We spend the most money of any group of people. These guys will turn around, we're Black, turn around and our agents will tell us, don't go back into your own community and invest. . . . They work for us. We don't work for them. The government is not going to give us jobs . . . we gotta do it ourselves. If a guy asks you to buy sneakers on that commercial, before you buy those sneakers or those football shoes or whatever, you check and see if he's running in your community first. You check to see if he invested in you and then to your kids. And if he's not, don't buy it. Don't buy it. Now, my last point is [about] ownership. We have *got* to own because ownership brings power. And right now, we're lacking that. We can speak all we want, [but] until we start owning in our own communities, we are going to be in trouble. The reason I got into the business was probably because Jesse Jackson, Sr., talked to me one day. He said, "Brother, you got to be more than just a basketball player." And I got to thinking, "You know, he's right." He said I got to go back in the community. I got with Maxine Waters, we decided to do something right here in L.A. and we took it from there. Brother Al Sharpton, the same thing. We have got to invest in our own people. See, we can have these meetings all we want to. But if we leave here and go out the same as we came in, this has done nothing. This has done nothing. And so I want you, as I do, when these brothers come walking and got the music up loud—and that's okay, and they go get the car, they deserve one or two cars, that's all right, we all do; once we make it, we deserve something to say, hey, we have arrived—but you grab them and you say, "What are you doing for us? What are you doing for your people? What are you going to do to help other young [Black] men and women make it, too?" And it's not about just running up and down that court. Because, trust me, [there is always] going to be some more Magic Johnsons and on and on . . . running up and down that court. But how many Michaels and Magics are going to make a difference in our communities? There's a reason that Michael Jordan and Master P was on that list [of *Fortune*'s 400 Richest Americans Under 40]. And you know the reason? You guys out here. Understand that. We set the trend, people. Why do you think white young kids wear their hats backward? We set the trend on everything. If it's cool in our community, it's cool in the suburbs. And so, my point is, we helped Michael and Master P get to that $400 mil. Now, only thing I want them to do is give some of that $400 mil to the Black community, because they're going to make. . . . They won't be the only ones with $400 mil if they invest in us. It'll be a billion. That, that's my point. And I gotta say this. You're gonna cut me off, I gotta say this, I gotta say this. Because, see, I don't want to be Magic Johnson, I don't want Michael to be Air Jordan and all that. When I walk into a room, I want to be Mr. Johnson. That's what we gotta strive for. Respect. See, it's about respect. That's all we've been talking about up here. We have got to respect Black people. That's it.

R. Brown: Danny Glover, the reason that you're here is that you've done something with your status as a cultural hero. Among the subjects you've chosen to focus on is AIDS. Why?

Danny Glover: We have to do the work that's necessary to ease whatever the pain is that exists here, this moment. Whether that pain reflects in terms of the prison system. Whether that pain reflects the number of underserviced African Americans with AIDS. Whether that pain deals with the number of the disproportionate number of African Americans on death row. Whether that pain deals with the disproportionate number of African Americans who don't have health insurance. The disproportionate number of African American children who live in poverty. I know that we have to deal with that now and that becomes critical at this moment. But what do we do about the future for our children, the future for the world? The future in how the world is going to look? When I went to the WTO, and Maxine was there, premeeting, preconference, I heard people talk about issues around food safety. I heard people talk about issues about an environment, that you can't go on under this incredible, this incredible consumption, conspicuous consumption that we go on. This whole idea of development only by how much we make or how much we spend, how much we consume. Those things began to hit to me, hit home to me in a different way. So we had to begin to look at the world in terms of affirming life itself. Native Americans talk about the earth and the Mother Earth. They're often the protectors of the Mother Earth. They talk about it. They've honored the Mother Earth unlike anyone else. Where do we stand in that? Where do we take, where our issues are right now, at this particular moment, confronting those issues? Let's deal with that. We got a lot of work to do on that level. But at the same time, at a higher, and

I'm sure Michael will say it on an even higher level in a moment, the moral level that I'm sure Dr. King talked about is that how do we form the world, how do we begin to construct the world that we want to see? We cannot just integrate for the sake of just integrating. We have to take a position that preserves the world for our children. Our children, yes, but for the world's children. The work on AIDS has been part of that. The work on AIDS is to say, let's look at the relationship between AIDS here with underserviced communities here in an African American community and those in Africa. You know, we can raise $20 billion for Kosovo, but we can't get a billion dollars, we cannot get a billion dollars for Africa. Which is not what we need. We have to clearly place ourselves in some sort of framework, and our dialogue not only has to be . . . I spent three days in Jackson, Mississippi, with Bob Moses. Here's Bob Moses teaching young African American kids algebra, because he believes that algebra is their passport to the future. He believes algebra is their passport to citizenship. And he's using rap teachin' 'em that. He's using their creative energy. So we gotta find ways of using that creative energy of young people. We've got an enormous job ahead of us. Not us just here on the panel talking about it. But that's going to involve you. That's going to involve you taking a stand and that's going to involve you. . . .

R. Brown: Les Brown, you deal with the inner self and questions of motivation. How do people go about dealing with that balance between the need to take care of themselves and the need to be committed to the larger community?

Les Brown: Well, I think that when you look at something that was said by Dr. Carter G. Woodson, "If you can determine what a man shall think, you'll never have to concern yourself with what he will do." That helping us to overcome the psy-

chic disrepair, helping us to begin to get a larger vision of ourselves and seeing that we can, in fact, make a difference, but
engaging in an ongoing process of healing ourselves. And I
think that a step in the direction is what we're doing right
now, talking about these things, looking at how we can begin
to develop closer relationships, not just now, but when we
leave here, and what value we can bring to each other and to
our communities so that as we begin this new century, we begin to develop a vision that we are literally involved in shaping
the future for generations yet unborn. We should have a mandate, a sense of oughtness, that we have to live with a higher
sense of responsibility and a sense of mission. That we have
some contribution that we ought to make and we can't do it
individually, by ourselves, that it takes all of us, collectively,
having a collective vision of where we're going.

Sharpton: The fact of the matter is, you can be the richest
Negro in L.A. tonight and still get pulled over in Beverly Hills.
Now, how we deal with empowering ourselves is by building a
collective wealth. The reason that what [Magic] Johnson is
doing is important is he's developing a wealth in our communities from coast to coast. Not just making him some money.
To act like we ought to look up to some guy 'cause they got
money is ridiculous. We don't know who was the richest Black
guy in Atlanta in 1963, but we know who Dr. King was 'cause
he stood for something. So whoever got money, doesn't mean
they stand for something.

Waters: For the last five days, I have been meeting with all of
the former gang members, gang members and hopeless young
people in our community, because we got a violence problem
here. It's real. And on Wednesday, based on some of the recent work that we've been doing, we have agreed, we have a

consensus among these young people, that they have to really tell America what they want and who they are and how they're feeling. . . . [We need to] stop being so afraid of our young people that we can't get past the fact that their pants are down here and the cap is turned here and the jewelry is around here. They are begging for us to support them, to understand what's happening with them, and they are smart. What they're basically [trying] to say is, instead of concentrating all your time on how you're going to lock us up, keep us longer, try us as adults, help us get some of the money and the jobs and the opportunities, Democratic Party, Black adults, community, everybody who's saying, "Why don't they go away, why don't they disappear, what can we do with them?" They're saying, "We want to work. We want a part of this prosperity."

Malveaux: We need to put this entire conversation about hip-hop in a context of the fact that young people have always been in older people's faces. I mean, in my day it was the platforms, the big Afros, I guess it's still the miniskirts. . . . But every generation has done that. So to begin to condemn young people because they're young is problematic. At the same time, we are in a peculiar place as a people. Danny Glover said something earlier about envisioning the world the way we wanted to see it. And I don't think that we do enough of that. We're stuck in this box where we make excuses for Black folks: "Oh yes, but look at all the pain, so they didn't have no choice but to go upside somebody's head and take they pocketbook." Not. Or you know, we make excuses for each other or we attempt to put it in context. Can we get out of that box? I mean, I think it's a box that we have to get out of, too, because it's a box of abuse of excuses. If we can envision a world the way that we want to see it, envision a kind of employment situation that we want to have, envision the kind of ownership opportunities that we want to create, then that can drive some of our public policy. If we don't envision things this way, we place ourselves in a box of constantly having to react, constantly having to make excuses: "Well, the Black man stole something, oh yeah, but they had too many people looking at him because he was Black." Well, you know we have too many Black elected officials that have been investigated, but guess what, some of them suckers did it. Now, not all of them. But some of them did it. And so let's be really clear that if we envision a certain kind of morality, a certain kind of ethics, a certain kind of integrity, if we begin to envision some of that, then we can drive our policy in that way. And then we don't get into this thing of "You're speaking pain when you callin' me a bitch because your pain is going to intensify if you do that in my face."

Kunjufu: We talk a lot about the fact that we earn $500 billion. But even that's too large. I'd like for all of you, for homework: What percentage of your check, forget the $500 billion, what percentage of your check do you spend with African American businesses? That's the first question. The second question: It makes no sense to work forty hours for somebody else and can't find two to five hours to volunteer and work in your own community. So the second question is: How many hours do you volunteer with an African American organization? Third, ultimately, our problems we've been discussing with regards to our youth, they are the result because we are the only race asking someone else to educate our children. Therefore, we need to put more pressure on public schools that educate our children, number one, and number two, we need to develop after-school, Saturday schools. We need rites-of-passage programs to develop our youth after school. But when we really get serious, we need to develop our own independent schools that will teach our children not only skills but a commitment to the race. This term "Black middle class," this 25 percent of our race that earns over $50,000 a year, if they do not live, spend, volunteer, invest, or contribute back to the Black community, what good is it to have that kind of class? Mr. Johnson [mentioned] the need to build institutions. I own a publishing company, I own a bookstore, I own an independent Black school, but here's my concern. As you know, Mr. Johnson, it is hard building institutions when your people hate themselves. Let me be clear. How can Black literature be hot—and Black bookstores and Black distributors and Black publishers be cold? How can a people spend all of their money with Borders and Barnes and Noble and Amazon [while] Black bookstores are hurting? So when we talk about $500 billion as Dr. Malveaux mentioned, there are some things we can't spend with each other. But when we talk about the soul-food industry, when we talk about the music industry or the book business, there are some industries [in which] we can make a difference when we get serious.

Crouch: I just wanted to say that I had left one thing out when I was talking about the Mandela business, which was the overwhelming significance of all of those Black mayors who refused to allow their cities to do business with companies that did business with South Africa. That was what put the final dagger in, because there were many, many mayors. Maynard Jackson [is] an example. When he built Hartsfield Airport in Atlanta, which was the biggest airport in the United States, he had all these guys who normally just gave the money to the white guys, right. All the shops and everything else. Maynard Jackson said this was not going like that. This is not happening again. [The whites] said, "We don't know anybody." "You will know somebody." "We're not connected to those guys." "You will get connected to those guys, right." Now the upshot of which is, when you go through Hartsfield Airport, you see something that you don't normally see in most airports in the United States. What you see [is] a lot of Black people who have business shops and stuff in the Hartsfield Airport. We have to remember one thing, and I told Peggy Noonan this once when I was being interviewed, 'cause I grew up as the proverbial "kid in a single parent household." She said, "Well, uh, that must have been difficult." I said, "Not as difficult as you think, because all of the Black guys in the community were surrogate fathers, you know." You were able to go to Mr. Michael, Mr. Danny, Mr. Les, Mr. Hugh to take care of you. We need just a renaissance of what the good old traditional Afro-American community was and we'll be all right if we do the business, the politics, and remember who we are. . . .

Johnson: We have to change our thought process. We've been conditioned to live for today. We have got to get out of that. The reason we're being left behind is because of that thought process. We have got to think ahead. The new Harlem USA Mall was built in Harlem. Do you know, now all white Americans are going into Harlem, buying up all the brown-stones. Because they know we gotta go back now. Harlem is being rebuilt. But we won't own it. You see. Because they know that's where it's going. People out here, listen to me. The money is going to our neighborhoods now. The suburbs is all built out. So we have got to pool together, put your dollar with another Black person's dollar, and on and on and on, and take a hold of our community.

Chideya: Our tribe has to be more educated, more advanced in order to succeed, and, as someone who personally runs a Web site called *PopandPolitics.com* that tries to throw some of these issues out there, I think that it can be. There's a newsletter out in the Bay Area called *The Electronic Drum,* and we can make the Internet our electronic drum that carries our voice forward. Educational tracking and educational segregation is one issue we have to keep a close eye on. And that ties back into the digital divide, because most of the Black children in America today still go to majority Black schools. Segregation has ended, but segregation lives on. And so when you talk about educational resources and when you talk about computers and wiring schools, you have to talk about wiring Black schools, and you also have to talk about where Black children are educated in majority white schools, because there are systems of tracking so that Black kids go into the vo-tech classes and white kids go into the computer classes. So, if you've got a kid in a majority white school, you have to make sure that they are getting into the classes that are actually going to teach them how to do HTML, how to be Web savvy, and not just into a class where they're going to learn how to do outdated skills from twenty years ago.

I'm someone who has lost family on both sides of the ocean. I've lost American family to AIDS, I have lost family in Zimbabwe to AIDS; my father is from Zimbabwe and 25 percent of the population there is infected with HIV. African Americans have always been the moral center of this country. We were during slavery, we were during Reconstruction, we are now. And if anyone is going to draw attention to this global holocaust of the AIDS crisis, which right now is centered in Africa but is moving through India, moving through Russia, it is us. We are the ones who are going to draw attention to the fact that these people do not have to die. That we have drugs that will treat people and prolong life. Life should not be dependent on your income. And that is exactly what's happening, right now. And so, and this is, this is not just about life in Africa. In Newark and in Jersey City, in New Jersey, about 2.5 percent of the African American population is HIV-positive. That is the same percentage of people that were HIV-positive in many parts of Africa fifteen years ago. We are setting ourselves up through the lack of drug treatment programs, through IV drug use, through the heterosexual transmission to women by IV drug users, through the birth of children who are infected, through transmission in the gay community in people of color. We need to think about our sexual practices, we need to be aware, we need to break the silence. Let's talk about this and let's do something about it and let's demand that the government treat us like people who deserve to have our lives saved.

One reason we may have this generational divide between the hip-hop generation and the civil rights generation is actually not just because of the fear, but because of the love. A lot of parents love their children so much that they didn't want to share their pain. They didn't want to share the pain of all of the racism that they bore the brunt of during the civil rights movement. They didn't want to talk about the jobs they were denied. They didn't want to talk about the apartments they didn't get. They didn't want to talk about the beatings. They didn't want to talk about the searches. And so children my age didn't hear about all the trouble that their parents got into and the things that they went through. And my family was very honest. My mom was like, "I didn't get this apartment and this man did this to me." And I heard these stories so when things happened to me, I had a context for it and I knew that I wasn't the first person in my family to face things. But there are a lot of people my age who are bitter, because they were told that life would be peaches and cream, and it wasn't. And I think that you cannot lie to kids. You cannot lie to Black and Brown children and tell them that the world is okay. It is much better to tell people about the problems of the world and give them a shell to protect them than to tell them that everything is okay and then let them get hurt.

R. Brown: Hugh Price, let me read just one sentence from your report called *The Technology Gap.* "The deeper problem is that many poor neighborhoods lack the infrastructure available in affluent areas. Groups such as the United Church of Christ, that have studied patterns in telecommunications investment, have found that all too often, television and cable companies have moved quickly to wire wealthier suburbs with advanced systems, while poor inner-city neighborhoods aren't upgraded. While public attention is often focused on whether individuals can get a service, the equally important problem is that lack of adequate telecommunications facilities makes an area less attractive for businesses." Now that's a structural problem and that's beyond "Go out and get a computer." How do we address that kind of structural impediment?

Price: Our children are being reared in communities where there aren't enough preschool facilities, but we know that high-quality preschool makes a huge difference. That needs to be a point of organization politically. Our children are being educated or being sent to schools, especially here in California, that are too big. Research says they should be smaller. Schools where half of the teachers that are teaching them science and math, which are leading-edge subjects, aren't even qualified to teach those subjects. . . . Schools, even advanced-placement courses in English and political science, where they're not even being asked to write. We need twenty-first-century schools for twenty-first-century children. And those are small schools, teachers who know their stuff and believe in our children, schools that are wired, not with the computer over in the closet, but schools [where] computers [are] everywhere.

Waters: We have got to stop being victims of a system that would deny us if we allow them to. We have got to get up parents, go to those schools, and demand that the system educate our children. We have discovered the most important ingredient in a child being successful educationally is the involvement of the parents and the community. There are increasing opportunities to close this digital divide, but we have got to stop buying $250 tennis shoes and clothes and buy a computer. We have got to put our resources in the direction that will give support to our children's education. What's the difference between driving a Cadillac and a Ford? Get the Ford and buy some computers and some books. Yes, yes, you know and I know, and we don't have to keep saying it, [that] every institution in America is a racist institution. And they're only going to do what we force them to do. So don't sit around expecting the white man to educate your children. It is not going to happen unless you decide, unless you decide that our children are going to be educated. We can create our own Saturday schools to supplement the public education. Someone told me, right here in Los Angeles, even after we had the education dollars and the money to make sure that there were books in every school, that there were not books in every school. And you know why we didn't know about it? Because the parents and the community were not in the schools seeing what was not there. I want to tell you, your teacher is only as good as you are. Our children's educational destiny is in our hands. What we do at home to support education, a place to study, books, computers, that's on us—in addition to forcing the system [to be responsive] and making sure the system is spending our tax dollars to educate our children. Let's stop moaning and groaning and take our schools back in our communities.

Kunjufu: I mentioned earlier that we're the only race asking someone else to educate our children. Nationwide, we are 17 percent of the children in public schools. We're only 4 percent of the teachers, and African American males [make up] only 1.2 percent. There are boys who have gone K-3, K-6, K-8, and have never seen, never experienced an African American male teacher. Of the 1.2 million brothers in jail, 91 percent of our brothers are illiterate. If we teach African American males how to read, we have a 91 percent chance of keeping our boys out of jail. Black parents and Black teachers used to tell Black children, "Boy, girl, the country's racist and if you want to make it here, you better score more than 80, 90, or 100; you better be the best." But with integration, we started lowering the standards. Many of our youth who are doing well in school are teased. Some brothers are called sissies and in some schools, if you're on the honor roll, mm, you're acting white. . . . If being smart is acting white, then how do you act Black? We have to change the paradigm.

R. Brown: What I might ask you, just to follow up, is: "How do we change the paradigm?"

Kunjufu: We have to inculcate our values into the peer group. One way is cooperative learning. Peer pressure doesn't have to be negative. We have to encourage our youth to study together. It's amazing how schools have these big trophies for the basketball and football players and then these little buttons for the debate team and the spelling-bee teams. We have to also change that paradigm as well.

R. Brown: Professor Dyson, what is it that people can take from this discussion that enables them to organize and to focus more effectively on these questions?

Dyson: Well, first of all, even raising the issue as a problem is a step in the right direction. Because I think that we have to acknowledge that we're living in a white-supremacist society. We know that the odds are stacked against us. But we know that we come from a great people, who have a history of overcoming the odds, who refuse, as Howard Thurman said, to reduce their dreams to the level of the event, which is their immediate experience. I myself [was] born poor and Black in the city of Detroit; my brother is now serving life in prison for murder, in a prison. I get a chance to go to Princeton to get a Ph.D. It's not because I'm good-looking or better or smarter than he is, it's because of my personal desire to do well, but also because there were some forces arrayed against him that [were not arrayed against me]. . . . We have to resist the temptation to think individualistically and think about the collective enterprise of Black America. We end up reinventing the wheel because we think, we don't know, we're subject to geographical mishap. This brother is over here doing something, this sister is over here doing something, but we don't recognize all of us are like an inchworm trying to make step-by-step by doing it. One of the glories of modern technology is that it allows us to create a truly global village where the Internet links up people doing something in Nigeria with somebody doing something in New York. And I think we have to take advantage of that. I think that, to me, one of the reasons I speak to young people and about them [is that] I don't uncritically celebrate or valorize them. I go into where these rappers [are]; they look at me and they think, "Well, you a light-skinned, curly-hair, suit-and-tie kind of Negro, what you know about hip-hop?" Right. And I break 'em off something proper, dust 'em off, and let 'em know what time it is. Then I say this. "I know your stuff, but what do you know about what I teach?" So I ask them, "Do you know Du Bois?" It takes high intelligence to create lyrics of the extraordinary poetic intensity that many of these young people do. The point is there's a larger community . . . and it's our responsibility to say this: You must not only learn what you learn in so-called hip-hop, but you must also pass the test of knowing the history of what produced you, that gave you the capacity to do what you do. We have valorized, lifted up, magnified and glorified our athletes and entertainers, and the best of them deserve that kind of magnification. But we must celebrate the dignity of the everyday. Those teachers who get up in the midst of difficult circumstances and teach those snotty-nosed kids, and give them a sense of love and support, you must embrace them.

Sharpton: I think that to go back to the question, how do we leave here, where do we go? One, we must really try to develop the mechanisms that Dr. Malveaux talked about in terms of bringing together our resources to build institutions as Mr. Johnson has done and support them. And the whole social fabric of our community from our churches to our educational institutions [should be geared] toward that support. Second, we must deal with public policy. We are sitting here on the eve of the Democratic Convention with no real tangible challenges before the nominees. There's an insult to lend a billion dollars to all of Africa to deal with AIDS. It is an insult that in the last sixty days, we've seen a man beat to death by police on live television in Philadelphia, a man choked to death in Dearborn, Michigan, over a $14 bracelet, another man killed by the state in Texas on one witness's testimony, and another man, retarded, killed last night by George Bush. . . . We cannot sit here and act like all is well. We are suffering from amnesia. We are acting like we got here without struggle. Our grandparents that had no money, no education, no political power, were able to raise us to be doctors and lawyers and judges. We're sitting up here with degrees on the wall, credit cards in our pocket, acting like we have no ability to do nothing but say, "Yes sir, no sir." We need to get up and we need to start fighting and we need to demand what is ours.

Malveaux: Some of the young people who are in school do not have functional parents. And this is a place where individuals can make a tremendous difference. People, we can advocate for any child. It doesn't have to be your child, it could be anybody's child. I think we need to start talking about going into these public schools and making them accountable. Making sure that the young person whose mother's sixteen or seventeen, who is intimidated by the structure, still has an advocate. It's not huge public policy, but it's one of the places I think we can definitely make a difference. Number two, my brother Sharpton, you know that I love you and have all respect for you. But I truly wish Black people would stop marching. Every time we march we go put our money in somebody's city and they get rich. We march, we holler, we scream, we yell, we come back, and we're in the same position. With all due respect, if a million people want to march, leave a dollar somewhere so that's a million dollars. If 2 or 5 million people want to march, leave something somewhere. I have no problem with gatherings. I like y'all as much as y'all like yourselves. But I really do have a problem with our need to have these events as opposed to doing something structural. And after the Million Man March, where the money, y'all? Remember, 10 percent was supposed to go to Washington, D.C. Where the money, y'all? Million Woman March, where the money, y'all? See there, Philly made a lot of money and they didn't even have a PA system. Now we have a Million Family March and this other march and I say march yourselves, march your dollars out of white folks' pockets. That's the kind of march I want to see somebody have. You know, march yourself to somebody's school. . . . I have over-marched, ain't gonna march no more, no more. You know. Number three . . . we waste our money as Black people. You know, we beg for what we need and spend on what we want. We go to white folks and ask them, come on, sit down, he's so cute, mmm-hum, okay. Beg for what we need, you know, and then we basically spend on what we want. We do not have control of our economic structure. You asked me the question earlier about the $500 billion and the answer is: That's our money. That's our money. We need to deal with it.

Bryant: There are so many of us who quite frankly don't care until it's our son that gets shot, until it's our brother that's in jail, that we have to go back to having a sense of community. Until all of us are free, none of us are free. The second thing is that we have to have an agenda. We have to stop doing drive-by events. We wait and become reactionary after something happens. We have to jump in front of it and say before it happens, we want to make sure that we can live up to what the Constitution is about. The third thing is that we have to make sure our actions speak louder than our words. We have become so quick to become massaged in our emotions that we leave out of here and buy some incense and some oils and say we're Black today and then we go back to business as usual and not go back on the front line. Make sure that the Democratic Party, that the Republican Party understands that Black people are not backup dancers. We have to make sure that they understand that the days of us just being tap dancers and dancers and basketball players are over, but this generation is engineers, and philosophers and teachers and maybe next time the vice president of the United States of America.

Chideya: I envision a future where Black people in America are not the only Black people. Where we see ourselves as part of a Diaspora, because I am a part of a Diaspora which includes people in Africa, people in Brazil, people in Mexico. I think one thing that has hurt us is that we feel very disconnected, and we are part of the majority of people on this planet. . . . It will help us to know our history, and there are so many great African American writers who have written about our history. There are so many great writers from so many other countries who have written about our history and we need to know a larger sense of that history. So first of all, let's know our history. You don't know your past, you don't know your future. And so let's learn our history, teach our history and place ourselves in that history . . . I see ourselves forging bridges throughout ethnicities here in America. My book *The Color of Our Future* talks about the fact that in fifty years, white Americans will no longer be a majority. And before we get to that point, we're going to go through a lot of strife and struggle. I think some of the hate crimes that we see in America today are part of the fact that we are in a period of change where there's a lot of fear. And we as African Americans need to be proactive, reach out to our Latino brothers and sisters, white, Asian American, Native American. We need to start building those bridges. We certainly need to follow all of the advice about economics and other empowerment, but we need to build those bridges and empower ourselves to be part of a larger Diaspora.

R. Brown: Thank you. Mr. Johnson.

Johnson: It's all about vision, That's what it's all about. Then second, it's all about a game plan. See, we never have a plan. Everybody's looking like, right now, today, like, "Well, what's our plan when we leave here?" The plan starts once you leave today, but also it starts in November. See, we know the issues. We could make a change starting with who's going to be the next president. Okay. But we gotta know, we gotta rally all together. We can't be divided, we got to stick together, we got to know, we got to demand. Okay, we want five, ten, twenty things and we want you, Gore, to uphold those twenty. And we want this person, whether it's Maxine, Rev. Jackson, Rev. Sharpton, we want you to lead to make sure we're going to get those twenty things. So we got to have a plan. And we can't be divided. Don't be fooled by it was eighty-five people, Black people and the Republican Convention, come on now. Don't be fooled by that. They didn't want us then, they don't want us now. Don't be fooled by Bush talking about he changed the state of Texas, talking about education. Yeah, he sure did, in the suburbs. Understand that. Understand, this time around, we got to have a plan for our people. And we got to make sure, you hear me, we got to make sure that Gore follows our plan. The Black plan. And if he doesn't, we won't vote for neither one of 'em. That's it.

R. Brown: Stanley.

Crouch: I think that everybody in here registering to vote, and voting, that would be a good start for something to do. Secondarily, I think that through churches, sororities, community organizations, voter drives can be hooked up. You know, a massive voter drive is never ignored. Strom Thurmond, who ran as a Segregationist in 1948 for president, with a Klansman on the podium with him, turned against his cut-buddy, Jesse Helms, on the Martin Luther King Holiday after Jesse Jackson went through South Carolina and registered a whole bunch of Black people. You can change a cracker, redneck, to go your way if his job counts on it. That's how politics works. It's not a matter of politicians liking you. You think when gangbangers go into emergency they care whether or not the doctors like them? They don't care if they like them. All they want you to do is get the job done. That's what we have to do. Get all the sentimentality out of the way. Have an agenda, push for it, and we have to make sure, finally, of that one long-term Afro-American conception that bettered our community and bettered the United States, because much of what is great about the United States is the result of our ancestors and of us. And never, ever forget that. Everybody else in the world seems to know that except us. There's an old Afro-American tradition, which is one of the highest forms of rebellion: It's excellence, excellence, excellence. If you become the very, very, very best at what you can do, as I was reared to do, then one thing for sure, you can get out from under all those stereotypes of being dumb, stupid, lazy, this and that. Shoot for the best. Be the very, very best. Pass that on to your kids and don't let them believe anybody who tells them that being dumb, backward, vulgar, and ignorant is being a real Black person, 'cause that's not true.

Price: Three years ago, I said in a speech that economic power is the next civil rights frontier. There are three elements to that. The first is economic self-reliance. Millions of our children are growing up poor. And that should be on the conscience of every Black person in this country. And the question is: What do we do about that? [We've] got to have world-class education, we cannot accept second-class education for our children anymore. Second, we got to push for economic parity. . . . All the economic vital signs, our unemployment rate, even though it's at record lows, is still twice the national average. Our homeownership rate, even though it's at record highs, it's still a third less than whites', so we got to push for economic parity so that our economic vital signs are the same. Thirdly, we've got to push for economic power, and that's the creation of institutions that we own and control and that don't just reach for the $500 billion market. We've got to create institutions that reach for the gazillion dollar market, all right, so that we really build wealth and it's from that that we get all the other political power and are able to finance our future. Lastly, I'd say that the twenty-five-to-forty-year-old generation of Black folks in this country is the most talented, best-educated generation in the history of our people and the question is: What you gonna do with that gift?

Waters: I think everything starts with the individual. And we've got to work hard on making sure that we're doing whatever we do with all the integrity we can muster. Every night when we go to bed, we've got to ask God to make us a better person, so that we can do our work with integrity and not be compromised. The biggest problem that we have is those people who have a platform for power are literally giving it away, throwing it away, compromising it away. We cannot get so friendly with corporate America that we can't take them on and boycott them. I know that our organizations and our politicians need money to run for office and to do civil rights work, et cetera. But if you're taking money from the major banks and financial institutions while they're taking our grandmama's houses in predatory lending, and you can't speak up about it, if you can't join in helping to fight for legislation that will make the Community Reinvestment Act real, so that we can stop them from making loans that they know people can't pay back and taking the homes and the equities out of our communities, then you're not doing your job with any integrity. It goes on and on and on. You cannot afford to say, "I can't move against Chevron, 'cause my friend is the vice president of Getting the Negroes Straight," or whatever it is they do in that corporation. You can't do this work without some measure of integrity. We have to accept responsibility for who we are. In the final analysis, let me say this—it's not what you do on the stage, it's what you do in the back room that counts.

Kunjufu: If we gave Congresswoman Waters and Congressman Jackson and the Congressional Black Caucus an agenda of certain issues that we want and we tell them that we are now organized enough to vote as a bloc and if you don't adhere to these three to four concerns that we have, then you will not see us in November, then you will see some changes made. That's number one. With regards to all of the construction contracts taking place in this city, and I've seen Rev. Sharpton do this in New York, if we shut some of these cities down, literally tie the city up, in other words, no longer just a march, I'm talking about a closing down—if you don't put us in, then we will simply shut you out. That's the second thing we need to do. Third, we all need to volunteer some time, we need to contribute some money. We need to develop after-school programs for our children. Build some independent schools. The next thing we need to do. If you think this is hard, the hardest thing you will ever do in life is to keep your spouse. We need to reduce the divorce rate in our communities. Stay married and take care of your children.

Dyson: I would suggest to us, as Black people who love Black people, that we've got to join our religious sensibilities and our political practices. When Congresswoman Waters talked about integrity, that is so very important, and if we're going to have integrity as leaders, we've got to be honest about something. When we talk about race and white supremacy as we do, and I do, as many of us do, we've got to admit as well that class is an equally problematic problem in Black America. What we've got to do is acknowledge that we have a responsibility. As Rev. Sharpton said, not only do we have amnesia, we have what I call Afro-amnesia. We've got Black forgetfulness about where we came from, how we got up, how we came to where we are, and what we've been able to do.

I want all of you to become Trojan horses. We can't romanticize what happened before integration, as if what happened before, when we had segregation, that it was all perfect—we know it was powerful, but it wasn't perfect. Because we had paper bag tests. Light-skinned elite got something, dark-skinned had to stay back. We know people who had money and cash had something, people who didn't have [any didn't]. I know I get into some places because I got that look. I'm a light-skinned, glass-wearing, curly-hair, suit-and-tie kinda Negro. But when I get up in there, I let all them other niggas inside of me out. Be a Trojan horse. All of those other "despised" people, take them with you.

ADVOCACY IN THE NEXT MILLENNIUM:
A Symposium

Afternoon Session

Professor Charles Ogletree,
  Moderator

Dr. Na'im Akbar

Danny Bakewell, Sr.

Dr. Johnnetta Cole

Nikki Giovanni

Professor Lani Guinier

Rev. Jesse Jackson, Sr.

Congressman Jesse Jackson, Jr.

Bishop Noel Jones

Randall Robinson

Iyanla Vanzant

Dr. Cornel West

Malik Yoba

Charles Ogletree: More than a century ago, W. E. B. Du Bois told us that the problem of the twentieth century was the problem of the color line. A problem we know about. We are here in Los Angeles in the twenty-first century. We are told it is the new millennium. There is a new economy. . . . But I think we still have some old problems. But what we need today is new solutions to those problems. And today, we have assembled some of America's most creative thinkers to talk about new solutions to the problems. . . . Dr. Cornel West, you wrote this book called *Race Matters*. . . . You opened that book by talking about one of the most significant events in our history. It happened right here in this state, right here in this city, that some called a "riot," some called a "rebellion," some called a "revolution." What do you see as the first step in the new paradigm, Professor West, that Black people need to deal with for the twenty-first century and the new millennium?

Cornel West: Well, I think first, we have to have a serious focus on vision. Where there is no vision, the people perish. And part of the problem today is that our vision of freedom has become narrow and truncated. If you go back to the Black freedom struggle, freedom was about Black self-respect, self-love, and control over our destiny. That's a fundamental ideal. These days freedom is much more [about] personal security, material prosperity, and trying to "get over." That's not freedom. That might be one aspect of freedom, but if that's all that the foremothers and forefathers fought for—just for some Black folks at the top to get over— then they struggled in vain. And they did *not* struggle in vain. So how do we incorporate the personal security and material prosperity but at that deeper level, self-respect, self-love, treating others right, unifying in such a way that we agree to disagree [while] still trying to redefine the dream for, not just America, but the world. 'Cause America's conception of its dream is just freedom to succeed to get over. That's too narrow and there'll never be enough spaces at the top for all Negroes to get over. Never. You got to have something broader. And that's true for brothers and sisters of whatever color. . . .

Nikki Giovanni: I really think that the most important thing that the Black community could do right now is, we have to support the right of prisoners to vote. They are citizens, they have duties and responsibilities. We have duties and responsibilities to them. If, for example, prisoners voted in, ah, North Carolina,

Strom Thurmond might be gone. . . . Somebody said [to me], "Well, Nikki, these people committed crimes." But a lot of the crimes they committed, if they could vote, wouldn't be crimes. And I write to prisoners. . . . I have a friend in Marion, Illinois, maximum security. Whatever he's done, he's not coming out. But he still wants a playground for his little Black granddaughter. He still wants a decent school, he still wants a hospital. Somebody [asked me], "Well, how will we handle this if we let prisoners vote?" But these are men who we say we want to rehabilitate . . . and we say we want to keep them involved in being citizens and being involved with us. They need to exercise their right to vote because whatever crimes they have committed do not relieve them of the responsibility of being citizens. It's an important thing. Lani was talking about responsible democracy. That's it. These men and women are a part of us. They have the time and the energy to be involved with us on a daily basis. . . . I don't know what a felony has to do with voting. I just don't. . . . Some of these people are wonderful and some of these people are awful. But they are still citizens and they have to be treated with the respect of any other citizen and people have to talk to them as if they were citizens. They are not things . . . they are human beings and we have to be involved with them.

Ogletree: Professor Guinier . . . you were talking recently about a *New York Times* front-page story that [stated] that there are 2 million men and women in jail today. Many of them are African American. . . . Have we made a mistake the way we have disenfranchised African Americans who are in the criminal justice system? . . . How should we look at the justice system differently . . . ?

Lani Guinier: I think the new paradigm has to be a paradigm in which people of color are leading in a fight for justice, not "just us." And this is a paradigm in which we lead and other people join us in this fight because we have a vision that will make America better, not just for us, but for all people. To answer your question specifically, and in the context of criminal justice, that means we have to fight against the War on Drugs. The War on Drugs is a war on Black and Brown people. It is not a War on Drugs. There are, since 1990, 7 percent more people in prison. Since 1990, that means eight of those ten years were under the watch of a Democratic Administration. This is a war being fought by both political parties against the Black community. We criminalize drug use for Black people and we medicalize it for white people. And if you go to a drug-treatment center, 60 percent of the people in that center are white. If you go to a federal prison, 60 percent of those people in there for drug possession are Black or Brown. . . .

Ogletree: Rev. Jackson, you have been talking for a long time about this issue of justice and racial profiling. . . . You've written books about it, you've given speeches about it, the whole Wall Street Project's about it. . . .

Jesse Jackson, Sr.: I'm a Baptist preacher and so we start low and rise slow. Rise high, strike fire, and sit down. I think that, if I can take a step back, why have the Williams sisters and Tiger Woods and football, basketball, baseball, track, boxing, why are we superior in those areas, with the least amount of equipment with which to practice? Now, we have seen so many great athletes lately, we act as if it's natural and not honed science and skill. When you run up and down the basketball court full speed and you have many options and you make the right option, hoist a ball through a cylinder, you're making some geometric decisions. Very scientific. Everybody can't do it. We're the best in the world at applied geometry on that court. Even we have become accustomed to seeing it as natural as opposed to a work ethic. Why are we the best at that? Because whenever the playing field is even, and the rules are public, and the goals are clear, we excel. Now, that drives me to the issue of equal protection under the law. . . . In slavery, we did not have protection under the law. In legal segregation, we didn't have equal protection under the law. And what made Dr. King's leadership superior was, his leadership did not just focus on faith and spirituality and private self-esteem, but on changing the law. His movement made it illegal to deny us access to equal protection. And August 6, last Sunday, was the thirty-fifth anniversary of the right to vote. . . . We now have the power to determine the next president and the next Congress and the next Court. We have that power, if we have the vision to demand the right thing with that power. . . . Now, my other point, [which] will tie in with Lani's, is this. This is a hard one for us to get to. I know it's hard. . . . I'm going to invest in a resource struggle for our share of resources. The reason why is, it's not just Black— most poor people are not Black in America. They're white, female, young, and invisible. And most poor people are not on welfare, they work every day. Lani's point is that if we see that vision, we can lead the nation. We must believe we have the capacity to lead the nation, not just the neighborhood.

Iyanla Vanzant: I confess that I am not politically astute. I'm not. I don't know who's on what committee. I don't know what they are voting on. I don't know none of that. This is what I know. I know what I look at. And what I see. And what I see is a country in which one of the greatest miracles ever to take place, which is the birth of an individual, where a sperm meets an egg in darkness and becomes a Cornel West. That's

deep. That's deep. I see the greatest miracle in the world being ignored and denied every day. When human beings are not
born to know that they are worthy. That they're just worthy.
There must be something really, really wrong with you to
think that God would make you unworthy. To make you that
way. And we live in a society where people are born to believe
they are unworthy. In the new paradigm, I don't know if we
need to have welcome parties in the maternity ward, I don't
know if we need to set up signs, but [for] every being born,
somebody needs to just look at 'em and say, "Welcome, I'm
glad you're here." That's number one. Number two . . . we got
to take God out of the closet and put God square in the
center of our lives. Let me tell you what I mean when I
say God. . . . When I say God, I mean the highest vision of
who you are; put that in the center of your life. When I say
God, I mean looking at who you are, your cellulite, your little
bit of hair, your crooked teeth; look at that and say, "Damn,
look at that, ain't that good." That's what I'm talking about. I'm
talking about being able to get up in the morning and know
because you've already been welcomed into the world that
you are worthy, simply because you are alive, that whatever
you do that day is important to the entire universe. That's the
God I'm talking about.

Ogletree: Brother Malik Yoba, in the twentieth century and into
the twenty-first century, we've always defined young people,
particularly Black young people, and particularly Black males,
in negative ways. Drugs, crimes, gangs, that's the paradigm.
And whenever we see them on television, hear them on radio,
it's about, you know, it's about crime, it's about all these other
things, and maybe we've made a mistake by not focusing on,
talking to and understanding and communicating with young

people. . . . What do we need to say, what are we not saying, to connect with the young people, men and women in our communities?

Malik Yoba: Question. Anyone in the room twenty-five and under? Okay. Hold on. Let's go a little higher than that. Forty-five and under? Next question. How many people volunteer their time? Okay. So that's a healthy majority. Personally, I think that you know I'm thirty-two years old, I got shot at the age of fifteen. From the age of seventeen, I've been committing my life to community service. Most folks know me as an actor. What most folks don't know is the commitment I've had to communities around this planet. I think that it's just about being a proactive, productive citizen. You know, taking your highest self, putting it front and center in your life, and recognizing that you have a purpose. For a long time I would do a workshop with young people, and I've done it in South Africa, in South America, in the Caribbean, in Rikers Island and Beverly Hills. And the workshop was called "Why Are You on This Planet?" At no point in my education was I asked that question from teachers, from my peers, you know. I think that it's about holding firm the idea that we must live purposefully. That we must put our spirituality back where it's supposed to be. See, young people, we make *Thong Song* go to number one. We do that. You laugh. But the number-one song in America was a song about a piece of underwear. Number-one song is a song like *Big Pimpin'*. Okay. We do that. . . . It's an interesting dichotomy, because on one hand our creativity, and I believe that artists are agents of change, our creativity, the younger generation allowed 70 million strong to grow up on hip-hop, which allows *Scary Movie* to make $142 million. That's hip-hop that did that. That showed the white kids, the

Asian kids, the Latino kids that it's not that deep anymore. Johnnetta Cole said to me backstage, and it's the first time I heard this from someone of her generation, she said, "Malik, my generation is in so much pain, because we want to know that the work we have done is not in vain." I said, "Well, maybe a place that we can start to create this new paradigm is to have more dialogue, intergenerationally." A couple days ago, I had a spiritual reading, and I don't mean to be too long, but I've struggled being an artist. Because I know that in this town, there's not a lot of love for us. So the question becomes: "What kind of love do we have for ourselves?" And this reader said to me the other day, he said, "Malik, you have the ability to convince a bunch of strangers to go into a dark room for two hours and take them on a journey and make them laugh, make them cry." And for the first time in my eight-year entertainment career, I began to own, on an artistic level, see I've always owned my artistry on an activist level, which is why so many people do know me, which is why I'm up here. People think, "Well, what's, Malik, *New York Undercover,* what's that about?" The reason is, I'm this lineage. And I understand it and I walk it. For me, as a young person, the biggest thing that I've embarked on—I had a daughter two years ago—is fatherhood. I played a dad on *New York Undercover,* I just did a national play where I had an opportunity to play a dad. I had a very unfortunate custody battle and during that process, I realized how much is lacking for men. So me, as an individual, right now, my commitment has been to responsible fatherhood. I believe that men, I believe that fathers are an emerging market. And I believe that we can be sold the value of responsible fatherhood through music, through television, through writing. . . .

Ogletree: Dr. Johnnetta Cole . . . you are the spiritual leader of higher education. What you did at Spelman, not just at Spelman, but for every student of color going to college, you've made it possible to be successful. And now we're changing those images. In the new paradigm, how do we get young people from birth to think of education as empowerment and to avoid some of the traps that Malik Yoba talked about?

Johnnetta Cole: I'm going to say that if in the process of honoring education, we could remember some old-fashioned stuff, I'd be mighty happy. I would be mighty happy for us to remember that education doesn't just hang, that it is a part of a system, and that what goes on in that classroom and does not go on in that classroom is tied to the way that this society of ours is organized. It is programmed and, unfortunately, until we stop it, it works. I ask us to remember as we flirt with vouchers, with choice, with charters, with all of this stuff, that fundamental education is the belief in a child's ability to learn. It is, indeed, the outrageous, radical notion that every child is educable. And that, indeed, teacher expectation is the surest thing for student performance. While we flirt with all kinds of new things, to remember that parental engagement doesn't just come when you decide to take your child and put that child in another school. You can be engaged in the old school. But . . . we must continue to look at the United States and the way it is organized and to understand things systemically. To understand a system. You quoted our brother, W. E. B. Du Bois. We all quote him: "The problem of the twentieth century is the problem of the color line." Read the rest of the passage. He talked about that dividing line between the haves and the have-nots. That is systemic. We've got to address it.

Now, brother Professor Cornel West knows how much I admire his mind and his soul. We will focus on race. We will focus [on the fact] that race matters. But gender matters, too. The issue of Black women in this nation of ours cannot be solved by a race analysis alone. And so I'm asking that when we look at race, we remember to look at class, we remember to look at gender, we understand the nature of an American capitalist system that has put us in a given place. Let us understand our ability to change that through our own activism. . . . The well-educated person not only understands the world better but acts to make the world better. That's the ultimate old-fashioned notion of education.

Ogletree: Thank you. Congressman Jesse Jackson, Jr., you kind of stood at your father's knee and watched all of the great things he's done for the nation and the world, and you could have had a great life just simply being . . . a child of Jesse. But you said that wasn't enough. You ran for Congress. You've been elected with overwhelming majorities. You've sponsored legislation. You've even had the audacity to disagree with your father on some central issues about where this nation and this world should go. You've had some willingness to disagree with other Democrats, Black and white, about what we should do. And you have had the audacity to say, "We're going to get beyond platitudes and get to business." Can you tell us, from your point of view . . . what we should be focusing on right now in the new millennium?

Jesse Jackson, Jr.: Well, let me start by saying that we need a clear understanding on what is wrong with the old paradigm. . . . The old paradigm is '60s, 1960s, as a frame for organizing, when the new paradigm, at least from my perspective, should be from the 1860s as the basis for organizing. You see, 1960s organizing has us turning *on* each other . . . rather than to each other. And it manifests itself in this way: "Jesse ain't doin' what Martin did"; "Are you with the Martin side or are you on the Malcolm side?"; "My pastor is preaching in the church, but ain't doin' nothin' in the community." It manifests itself in us turning on each other and analyzing ourselves against an historical standard, rather than turning to each other and looking at the nature of the problem. And that problem is not in the 1960s, that problem is in the 1860s. Dr. King, who stood firmly in the '60s, did not look to the '60s for organizing, he looked to the 1860s, the nature of the problem. And in the 1860s at the conclusion of the Civil War, when two sides of white people came to fight and to blows over our question—"What to do with slavery and what to do with the newly freed slaves?"—it left us at the end of that fight with 620,000 Americans dead. More Americans died in that period of the nation's history than any other period and all other wars combined. That period, over our question, left us with no longer Democrats, Whigs, and Tories, it left us with Democrats and Republicans. And in response to the question of what to do with the newly freed slaves, the radical Republicans argued that we needed to invest more money in their education, their health care, and in their housing. The racist Democrats of that era made the arguments that those Negroes need to pick themselves up by their own bootstraps. The moderates argued that they needed to do something in the interim, and it ultimately became Reconstruction. And so the race paradigm is Democrats, who consider themselves liberal on economic issues but moderate on social issues; Republicans, who consider themselves conservative on economic issues but moderate or liberal on social issues. In other words, it is not our problem, it is the comfort that they find in the labels that they ascribed to themselves for not addressing the fundamental issues that remain front and center for all Americans. Now, that's their problem and it doesn't have us fighting each other as leaders. It has us analyzing them and telling them what we expect out of their historical failure for the last 140 years to deliver for all Americans, to deliver for all Americans upon their basic citizenship rights. Now, '60s organizing leads us to new programs. New laws, improvements on civil rights laws, affirmative action protection, it leads us to voting rights laws, and it leads us to public accommodation laws. Hundred and forty years of that. The solution is not solely in new laws; yes, we need new laws, but we need fundamental rights. Let me make this clear to you. Is America better, not only the African American community better, because of the passage of the Thirteenth Amendment that freed the slaves? Not only is our community better, but I would hasten to say all Americans are better. Is our community solely better because of the Fourteenth Amendment? Not just our community, all Americans have benefited from equal protection and the Due Process clause. I would hasten to say . . . not until we have the right to a public education of equal high quality, the right to health care of high quality, the right to decent, safe, and affordable housing, the right to safe, clean, and sustainable environment, the right to jobs in the form of full employment—[all] in the form of amendments to the Constitution, which not only will improve our common lot, but will guarantee for us and our posterity, for all Americans, true balanced economic growth, with a legal remedy when Democrats and Republicans fail to provide it for us. That is the new paradigm for progress.

Ogletree: Bishop Jones . . . we've talked about spirituality, we've talked about economic survival, we've talked about political involvement, we've talked about education. From your point of view, from the point of view of the clergy, [with] hands in the community every single day . . . what's your angst, your anxiety, your concerns for our community? What do you want us to be working on, to be thinking about, to be taking some action on?

Noel Jones: I see the psychological effects of all the processes, of politicizing all the processes of the economic systems . . . I wanted to keep that in mind by [offering] a quote from W. E. B. Du Bois in 1903 and then giving you a quote from 1982 by our just-honored colleague Brother Cornel West. . . . [Du Bois] says, "When you deal with a Black man, he's in an American world and it's a world which yields him no true self-consciousness, but only lets him see himself through the revelation of the other world. It is a peculiar sensation, this double consciousness, this sense of always looking at oneself through the eyes of others. Of measuring one's soul by the tape of a world that looks on in an amused contempt and pity. One ever feels his twoness: an American, a Negro. Two souls, two thoughts, two unreconciled strivings, two warring ideals in one dark body, whose dogged strength alone keeps it from being torn asunder." Now, eighty years later, Professor Cornel West says this: "Afro-American philosophy expresses a particular American variation of European modernity that Afro-Americans helped shape in this country and must contend with in the future. While it might be possible to articulate a competing Afro-American philosophy based principally on African norms and notions, it is likely that the result would be theoretically thin. . . . The life worlds of Africans in the

United States are conceptually and existentially neither solely African, European, nor American, but more the latter than any of the former." The significance here is that eighty years later we have the same essential concept and that is: We're African American, trying to blend into a society that's trying to make us helpless and useless. Consider the difference [between] . . . crack cocaine [and] powder cocaine. Powder cocaine, you slap the [user on the] wrist because you regard the powder cocaine users as useful. The crack cocaine users, you put them away for year after year, because you regard them as useless. So now their uselessness only becomes usefulness when you begin to privatize prisons. . . . The question has to be: What is the underlying spirit that controls policy-making in America? Is it money? And if it is money, is money then racist, because we came here to make money for the other side. . . . Nobody is going to do this for us. Nobody is going to fix this for us, Republican or Democrat. We have to fix this ourselves. We have to fix this ourselves. . . . The thing is, how are we going to express God as we live here? Nobody can have an experience with God and not feel good about themselves. When I feel good about myself, I take care of whatever looks like me and that starts with my children. Change the children. And that's our responsibility.

Na'im Akbar: Where do we need to go? We need to begin to understand that the solution to our problems requires us to generate self-advocating think tanks. Whereby, we no longer put all of our energy into trying to understand how to respond to someone else's agenda for us, but to begin to formulate an agenda rooted in a fundamental understanding of who we are. I am no longer of the opinion that we need to simply be concerned about analyzing other people's projects. Those projects are clear and predictable. What we need to do is to begin to engage, as Bishop Jones said, in understanding who we are. Who we are and understand what we need. What does that mean? That means that we must be very clear that our definition of who we are has not come from us, it's come from those who didn't want us to be anything but their property. What does that mean? It means that education is not simply learning how to read, write, and do quantitative analysis, it has to do with being able to understand who you are and what kind of potential that's buried into your very being. Education means you have to learn to not only be able to get a job, but to be able to understand how to build institutions to take humanity to another plane altogether. It means that. We must bring together the best minds we have, stop competing with each other, stop letting our egos get in the way. Listen, stop worrying about who's the best and who's the worst, who's at Harvard, who's at Morehouse, who's at Spelman, who's at Berkeley, who's at Stanford, who's at Florida State, and start worrying about all of us on the damned plantation and how we're going to get off of it.

Ogletree: Danny Bakewell, eight years ago, something happened to a brother named Rodney King. And folks said, with sincerity, "No justice, no peace." And we saw the justice system work, or not work, in the Rodney King case, we saw this movement to rebuild L.A. It sounded just like we heard in 1965 about rebuilding Watts. And I'm wondering, it didn't happen in Watts, it didn't happen in South Central, it may not happen this week. How do we go about rebuilding African American communities?

Bakewell: I ain't no preacher and I ain't never wrote no book. But let me tell you what I know. . . . What happened, it was not, it clearly wasn't a riot, it was a revolt. It was a rebellion by people who have been suppressed for 400 years and are still being suppressed today. Now we have a situation where, you remember Rodney King, but today, we remember Margaret Mitchell, Tyisha Miller. There are so many names that I could rattle on, it becomes startling. But the first thing we have to do is define the new paradigm in our eyes, by our definition, by our vision. . . . What I know is that every day we seem to cry for everybody and we take up everybody's cause, but nobody cries for us. Nobody cries for our children when they're shot down in the streets like dogs. Nobody is really educating our children. When we go back to fundamental education, we were taught by Black people. Most people up here, and we could read, we could write, we could phoneticize, and we wasn't hooked on phonics. We was just hooked on each other. And parents that drove home the fact that we had to do something or they were going to take it up with us. Those are the kinds of things that we have to do. We've got to stop criticizing these brothers who are rappers. 'Cause they own those companies. We've got to stop talking about these gang members. These are not gang members, these are our children. These are our brothers. These are our sisters. These are the ones that we have to make a way for. We've got to make a way out of no way. We are seeing a proliferation of people talking about retribution. . . . Who cries for our people? Who remembers our ancestors? Those are the kind of challenges we have in the new paradigm. Because everybody cries for everybody, but nobody cries for us.

Ogletree: Randall Robinson, a lot of people who don't know you have described you as an angry man. Every time Randall speaks, he is raising hell about something. Started in Virginia, took it up to D.C., then you went international with South Africa. You were angry and you brought thousands of people to Washington, D.C., in the '80s, to get arrested, to go to jail, to free Nelson Mandela. . . . But what people don't know, you saw the craziness going on in Haiti and our crazy backward foreign policy and you went on a fast. What people don't know, Randall came within hours of dying through this fast. That's the ultimate sacrifice, the ultimate struggle. I know you're not beholden to political parties or politicians. I've read all your books. You talk about Black people and white people. You talk about people who are rich, but one of the things we haven't heard today is the sense that this is not just what's happening within these fifty states, but if we want to really be effective, we can't just act locally, we have to think globally. . . . When we talk about education, when we talk about reparations, our history, our sense of pride and our sense of identity stops at the national borders. W. E. B. Du Bois talked about the problem of the twentieth century [being] race, but he also died a brokenhearted man, not here, but in Africa. He's buried in Africa. What do we need to do to think about the new paradigm when it relates to African American people realizing that it's not just South Central, but it's South America, South Africa, and worldwide?

Randall Robinson: On my next birthday, I will be sixty years old, and for those of us who have done this kind of work for a long time, when you reach a certain age, you begin to take something of a backward measure of what you have accomplished and where you have failed. And so, I think a fair starting point for transition to another generation of leadership would be to talk about how to build upon those things at which we failed. We've had episodic accomplishments that are important. But we shouldn't allow those things to eclipse in our own assessment of ourselves what is still terribly wrong inside our community that is so terribly disabling for us. I do not believe that our traditional models of leadership will work for us from this point on. I do not believe in messianic or celebrity leadership. I believe that leadership must come from the breast of common people. And to do that successfully, people have to have information that makes them self-actualizing. My generation was not able to give you the information that you need. For there can be no empowerment without information. And those who would victimize us will never give it to you, because our ignorance is the major rock upon which this exploitation is constructed. I have always believed, Charles, that you can understand almost anything you need to know about global politics and global economics if you can follow the money. . . . We live in a corporate state, in a corporate world, and many of us have discovered that the Cold War was not fought because of any religious, constitutional, essential loathing of communism. It was fought in defense of global money. To do what it wanted to do, where it wanted to do it, and to exploit anybody who had value to those who held it. If you look at the global population as a hand, the thumb would be constituted of those who one time ran the global slave industry. Those who colonized, those who built multinational corporations, those who essentially run the world. The thumb in 1970 controlled 70 percent of the world's wealth. In the year 2000, the thumb controls 86 percent of the world's wealth. The little finger the least wealthy, or the poorest 20 percent in the world, the little finger in 1960 controlled 2.3 percent of the world's wealth. Today, it controls less than 1 percent of the world's wealth and it is falling. We get information without predicate, without context. Information that we can't interpret. We know that AIDS afflicts 30 percent of the people in many African countries. We know that Congo is a disaster now. It does not work. But do we know that it was President Dwight David Eisenhower who ordered the assassination of Patrice Lumumba? Do our children know that we, Democrats and Republicans, imposed that tyranny on those people? Do we know in the 1950s, Western biochemists in Congo, looking for a vaccine for polio, made a mistake that is all documented copiously in Edward Hooper's book *The River,* and AIDS is the result? Do we have any idea what slavery produced for some as an enterprise and produced for others as an endless poverty? Do we know that slavery continued on in neocolonialism? And went on in Jim Crowism, went on in dejure discrimination in the United States. Do we know that the era of this kind of exploitation ran from the beginning of the Atlantic slave trade until yesterday? If we are poor, do we know why? Do our children know that it has nothing to do with them? They are merely fodder in a machine. Cogs to be exploited. And so it seems to me that we can do very little in the world besides and beyond the episodic protests and success that we have had in careers like mine. Until all of us understand more about what happened to us. So that we will come to a time when we walk on the Mall in Washington and something will look unusual about it. We will look at the Holocaust Memorial and wonder where the American Holocaust Memorial is. We will look at a monument to Thomas Jefferson and wonder where the monument is to Denmark Vesey. Wonder where the statue is to Gabriel Prosser. Wonder where the statute is to remember John

Brown. We must remember, my friends, that history forgets first those who forget themselves.

Ogletree: How many have heard of the Dream Team? Who's on the Dream Team? Not basketball, the legal Dream Team? Nah, nah, see that, that's the modern [legal Dream Team]. . . . There was a Dream Team that most of you probably don't know about. To put this all in context, sometimes we have to go back to come forward. There was a sister, right here in this town, who was prosecuted for murder and subject to the death penalty. She was a professor at UCLA called Angela Davis. And she was so afraid of the American criminal justice system that she ran and hid instead of facing our justice system. And she was prosecuted, largely because she was Black and female and communist. And when she was ready to come to trial, she couldn't find lawyers who would stand up and say, "I believe that you were unfairly indicted and I'm going to defend you." But she had the true Dream Team. It was Howard Moore, a brother down in Oakland, California; it was a white woman by the name of Doris Walker; it was a young Black woman by the name of Margaret Burnham, who worked at the NAACP and was the former head of the National Council of Black Lawyers; and from here in Los Angeles, it was Leo Branton. And what they did is that, when they went into that San Jose courtroom, against all odds, a virtually all-white jury . . . and they came out with an acquittal of all charges of Angela Davis. . . . When we look forward to new paradigms, we sometimes have to look back to legends we never thanked for the work they've done. Please thank Leo Branton, who's here with us today. And before you leave, there are a whole lot of Leo Brantons in the audience; say thanks to those grandmothers and grandfathers and others who made it possible for

us to be here. . . . Rev. Jackson, how do we make this week a
week where African American people throughout the nation
should tune in? You're the main hit on Tuesday [at the
Democratic National Convention]. What's the message you
have to this audience, to say that we should still be concerned
about and invested in conventional politics? What's the message for this audience and these voters?

Jackson Sr.: Well, there is a scripture that grips me as I listen to
Noel and others. It is through all of this, we cannot afford to do
less than our best and survive. We cannot afford [less] once we
analyze our situation, hang our hops on the willows. Because
you can't make music when you lose your joy. You lose your joy,
you lose your power. You lose your power, you surrender. . . . I'm
trying to say this. That life is continuous frames. There are no
gaps. You can't jump from here to [there]. Life is a process. . . .
It seems to me that we became so angry in '68 we said, "Ain't no
difference between Humphrey White, Nixon White; ain't no
difference between Humphrey and Nixon. There was, however
incremental, because behind—if in this case, Gore and
Lieberman win, and we win the Congress, we reempower
Maxine Waters. And that matters. We empower Conyers to be
Chair of Judiciary Committee, that matters. Charlie Rangel
will [be] Chair of House Ways and Means, that matters. I think
empowering forty Black congresspeople matters. I think that
they will have an impact upon the next Supreme Court judges.
And so, to me, that matters. I will only say this in closing as we
look toward making these decisions. . . . Without equal protection under the law, without an even playing field, there are all
kinds of psychological, political, economic, sociological consequences. And so this issue, however conservative it may sound,
equal protection under the law is revolutionary. Because slave

masters did not want to afford equal protection under the law. The Golden Rule is the most revolutionary rule. 'Cause it's a one-to-one ratio. And oppressors don't want a one-to-one ratio. I mean there is something downright revolutionary to an oppressor about one-to-one. Because they know that when the field is even, that we have a chance at excelling.

West: Rev. Jesse Jackson, Sr., and I want to go to the same place. We want to be free. We don't just want prosperity and security, we want freedom, self-respect, self-love, and self-determination. That's what we want. And what that means is that we have the courage to tell people the truth about the Bushes and the Clintons and the Gores and the Liebermans. When I see the Clinton Administration, I see escalating incarceration of Black brothers and sisters. I see increasing wealth and inequality. I hear saxophone playing, but I don't see overwhelming jobs with living wage. . . . What they gonna do for Black people? What they really gonna do for Black people? And I'm not just talking about the professionals, I'm not just talking about the Black politicians; Bill Clinton does very well for Black professionals and Black politicians. What does he do for Black working people and Black poor people and especially Black children? That's a question that we have to raise. And we raise that in a collective and cooperative way. . . .

Bakewell: We're not saying, "Run, Jesse, run," we're now saying, "Win, Jesse Jr., win." Because I think, the reality as we go forward into this new millennium as Nikki talked about, Black men in prison, we have to advocate for them to have the right to vote in prison. Because they are still citizens. . . . We've got to make sure that we are defining how we use the power that we have as we go forward, and certainly we need to send a loud and clear message: "If you don't respond to our issues, we will not respond to you."

Vanzant: It just makes me very, very nervous, because [those in power] are liars. And we know they lie. They have lied to us over and over. You know, Maya Angelou said, "When a person shows you who they are, believe them." They have shown us that over and over and over. It's like with my grandson, as long as I threaten to beat him, he will test me. But when I get the belt and start moving in his direction, he gets real clear that I mean business. So I say here, not just demand, not just tell them what they're going to do and accept, because they've shown us their dishonesty. We got to be willing to put something on the line. We got to be willing to put something on the line. To let them know, that from our highest self, we know we are worthy of you not only telling us the truth and respecting us, but doing what we have asked you to do for our own common good. . . . I don't think we should threaten them with the vote. But I also think that we shouldn't give 'em the vote. The question is: What's Plan B? Where is our Plan B? Where is it? And that's what we need to be working on.

Ogletree: We have the Rampart Division's police officers involved in maiming and hurting and injuring and assaulting, fabricating evidence on individuals. We've had the Diallo shooting. We've had the shooting of, uh, of Patrick Doresmand. We've had a lot of other attacks in the community. . . . What must we do as a community to address the criminal justice issue? There seems to be the same sense that we have to make a choice. That we either want safety on the one hand or we want liberty. That we have to make that dichotomy. Why do we have to sacrifice so much and why are we such targets in the criminal justice system?

Cole: May I just make one point that connects much of our conversation today? In focusing so much attention on the national elections, we remove our concern and our engagement with voting and decision-making on a local level that affects our lives every day. Including what you have just raised. You see, I don't have trouble making a connection between schools that do not teach our children well and prisons that are waiting for them. I don't have any trouble making connections between how we go for local elections and who the police commissioner is. And so the notion of our removing ourselves from participating in a process that chooses who will do us in is insanity. Fannie Lou Hamer's spirit will come and whoop us! Because that shero knew that that right was not simply the exercising of some academic process. That it affects the lives of human beings who are Black. And so I ask us to participate on local levels, who's on that school board, who's voted to be the commissioner of police, who is in the mayor's seat, who is making decisions that affect our daily lives.

Ogletree: Professor Guinier, people use the term "racial profiling," people complain about being pulled over, being targeted by police, and one of your views is that that might not be the right paradigm when we talk about the criminal justice system to focus on racial profiling. What's your view about that?

Guinier: I do not think that racial profiling is the result of aberrational rogue cops. Racial profiling is an official policy that was promoted by the Drug Enforcement Administration as a way of trying to interdict drugs into this country. Until we move beyond just the symptoms to look at the structure that makes behavior predictable, we will be focusing simply on individual-by-individual cases. So I want to go back to the idea that I started. We as Black people have to be prepared to lead a fight for justice, not "just us." And in fighting for justice, if we were to take the money that is going into the War on Drugs and put that money into the community, not just the Black community, but of course the Black community too, put that money into higher education. California, for example, used to have the premier higher education system in this country. Since 1995, California has been spending more money on prisons than on higher education. A first-year college professor here in California makes $41,000 a year. A prison guard makes $51,000 a year. So racial profiling is part of the War on Drugs and the War on Drugs is fueling this need for more and more prisons. We have to mobilize against the *system* that is creating the problem, not just the symptom that makes us see the problem.

Robinson: This responsibility for these kinds of problems has to be broadly shared by all of us, not just those who would lead us and seek our votes. When I used to work for Charlie Diggs, I worked for Charlie for two years. He was the senior member of the Congressional Black Caucus. In those two years, I don't recall a constituent calling us about any policy matter. And I don't recall Charlie printing so much as a button for his re-election campaigns, because he took his own constituency for granted. I remember a member of the Black Congressional Caucus telling me he was opposed to voter registration because he had all the voters he wanted. And believe me, this is not a peculiar sentiment. . . . Democracy has less to do with voting and more to do with what you do after you vote. I don't know why people think that Black politicians are supposed to be peculiarly virtuous. If you don't make them account [for their actions], they will behave as freely as anyone else would. And we don't do that. I'm not making any particular brief against the Clinton Administration. But I do know that there are at least 100,000 Rwandans dead because Madeleine Albright withdrew the peacekeepers. And I do know that there was no great howl from our community, or it would not have happened. I do know that tiny democratic Caribbean economies are now collapsing because of this Administration and its receipt of a million dollars from Chiquita Bananas to displace those Caribbean countries in the European market. I know that. People in St. Vincent are ingesting insecticide, farmers killing themselves because . . . this president has destroyed the economies of the democratic Caribbean. I do know that Black youth are six times as likely to be arrested for a serious crime as white youth. More likely to be tried and when they are convicted, they will serve twice as long for the same crime. Now, if there is a meeting between any elected official and Clinton, and anybody else in the Administration—any candidate seeking office—and these issues do not come up, then we have to accept responsibility. But first, we have to make sure that those we send to Washington do what we sent them there to do. . . . Mel Reynolds, Jesse's predecessor, in exchange for a photo opportunity with the president, voted for NAFTA. That's all. "What do you want?" "I just want a picture, Mr. President." Something's wrong with that. And what is wrong with it has to be shared by all of us. You demand nothing, you get nothing.

Jones: I hope we don't leave here feeling so discouraged about doing anything that we just don't do anything. Because apathy is one of our greatest problems. We have a power base. Each one of us in here must understand how significant we are as individuals. And if we collect those individuals together, we can move some things. . . . It's our sons, our nephews, who are being swept away by the system. So, until we begin to change the structure, what do we do with our nephews and our cousins and our sons in the meantime? I think we ought to institute in our own families and with faith-based organizations those kinds of things that would help to eliminate the vulnerability of our children. . . . I think we ought to demand of our pastors and our leaders the kind of programs and situations that will help make our lives better. Not only politicians.

Akbar: I know that [Randall Robinson] will address this, but there's a part of the reparations issue that I think is really crucial—because Bishop Jones talked earlier about the whole psychology. And I believe very firmly that the foundation of our greatest madness is rooted in the perpetuation of a slave's mentality. So the chains, the psychological chains of slavery, [are] the most debilitating mentality within our community. So all of the divisiveness in our communities, our inability to work to build our communities, our opposition to building institutions, our dependency on other people's directions, all of those things are a direct consequence of being incarcerated by the slavery mentality. So reparation, I really believe, even though it is a political and economic kind of demand—I think it must begin with us doing reparative work on ourselves. One of the problems is that we have not as a community acknowledged the reality of slavery. And since we haven't acknowledged the reality of it, we have not dealt with the devastation of it. One of the reasons the Jews can demand of the world to pay them up is because Jews understand what happened to them and they don't mind letting the world know about it. Listen, we apologized for slavery as if we put it on ourselves. We didn't enslave ourselves, contrary to what some of our scholars have suggested. Africans were not responsible for the devastation of slavery. Maybe we sold a few of our captives into the condition, but we had nothing to do with the devastation of what Marimba Ani called the "Maafa," the deep spiritual hurt that devastated our community. So, I would submit, I would submit that as a community, we must see reparation as a first step toward self-healing. We must know the hurt and the scars we still carry, because that begins to open up the door to healing and resolution.

Giovanni: I believe in great books. And one of the greatest books, in my generation, was *Roots,* because *Roots* really brought a whole nother thing and I've been carrying this because I want to share it with everybody: *Spirit Dive* by Michael Cottman, which is [about] the wreck of the *Henrietta Maria.* It was a slave ship off the coast of the Keys. It's the most important book since *Roots.* And I've been amazed that it doesn't make anybody's bestseller. That nobody's having him on to talk about discovering this ship. Because among the other things . . . we discover the little shackles. Because to hear about slavery you always hear it's grown men. I teach school and so I always ask my students, "How do you capture an elephant?" It takes them a minute. Because the first thing you have to do if you want to capture an elephant and bring him back to the zoo, you have to shoot the bull. Because the bull is not going to let you come in and take it. When the bull is dead, you then have to shoot the mother, because the mother is not going to let you take her son. The juveniles then take up the protection of the babies, because they're all that's left. So you have to shoot the juveniles. And what you get left with is the infants and the children. So you grab the babies and you carry them back and those that survive. And I submit that the wreck of the *Henrietta Maria,* this book, shows us that slavery was not about grown men and women being brought to America. Slavery was about destroying communities and bringing children. So I wanted to talk about that in reparations. I think Michael Cottman has the most important book in America and I think that we have an obligation to read it, to support it, and to know what he's doing.

Bakewell: The whole issue of reparations, I think, is extremely important for us as a community and as a people to digest. I remember, about a year or so ago, there was a sitcom, if you can believe this . . . called *The Secret Diary of Desmond Pfeiffer*. It trivialized the anguish and pain of our ancestors and the period of slavery. I mean, literally desecrated the bones of those who have gone before us. . . . It started out with two Black men being hung and somebody's laughing and saying, "I saw the urine screaming from their bodies." And no one, for a moment, spoke out on it. And one of the brothers or sisters sent it to my office so that we would see it, because it was the first cut. This community mobilized behind it, but let me tell you what was important behind that. What was important was that we, for the first time, even myself, began to really focus on how just immeasurable it is to try to comprehend slavery. It lasted 400 years. Just the courage and the strength of a people—which we never focus on, and people don't want us to focus on—to get to where we are today, is more deservant of reparations than any people in the entire world. And we've got to [hold] people accountable to that. The point Randall and I were talking about [is] this—the Holocaust lasted for 12 years, as compared to 400 years. That does not make it any less an atrocity. We must recognize it for what it is. But we must not allow other people to make their pain and suffering paramount and premier over that which our people have endured to get us here. I can't quote W. E. B. Du Bois, but I can tell you Fannie Lou Hamer is my sister and she said, "I'm sick and tired of being sick and tired." And that's what we've got to do with this issue of reparations. We've got to bring it to the forefront and force accountability on it.

Jackson Jr.: I was at a reception last night . . . and a young lady walked up to me, and I believe her name is Sharon; she reminded me of a . . . comment that I made about economic justice for all Americans. Not long ago, an African American in Texas was dragged to death behind a truck by three white men. . . . I had as many white friends who were horrified by that event as I did Black friends. As I'm sure all of us did. But then, I began to dream about another America. And not just focus on the racial insecurity of that event. I began to think of what would be different for that African American and those three young white men in Texas that could have changed the outcome. In order to do that, I had to look at what all four of them had in common. The first thing they all had in common is all four of them were unemployed. That's the first thing. The other things they had in common, all four of them had a high school education, the African American and the three white guys. If you remember correctly, the African American was hitchhiking on that day. He did not have transportation. That's an economic issue. Then I began to dream of an America, liken unto the ones that many of us who are sitting on this platform actually experience. . . . Because I have a house, I have a car, I have a good job, I'm going to be spending a considerable amount of my time this week working on the options that will be afforded Jesse Jackson, Jr., in that social and economic context. And that will determine whether or not I'm backin' that thang up this week or whether or not I'm on NBC, MSNBC, critiquing and analyzing what Democrats will be doing. Because those are my life options. Now imagine, if the four men, the African American and the three white guys, all had homes and mortgages to pay for. Imagine if all of them had a college education of high quality. Imagine all four of them having transportation. Imagine there were lights on that road as opposed to a dark road. Imagine if there were police on that road that night. In other words, imagine if there were economic security for those four Americans as opposed to economic insecurity and, therefore, racial insecurity. So the way out of the race dilemma for millions of Americans is economic security of the kind that many of us enjoy. I am not saying it's the panacea to all problems. But to systematically address the race problem and tensions over time, we should approach it that way. And lastly, let me just say this, if I might. On the issue of reparations. I am a proud sponsor of John Conyers's bill in the United States Congress. I would encourage, as I have encouraged, all members of Congress to cosponsor this bill. Some members of the African American Caucus cannot sponsor it. . . . Some members of Congress who are African American come from districts where 65 percent of their districts, even though they are members of the CBC, are white. . . . It's important to have that vote in Congress, to deliver on a lot of other things while we're trying to get reparations through. That's why it's important. But if their opponent uses the issue of reparations against them in their very local race, that would just be one less Negro in Congress. That's just a practical reality, because [the opponent] will tell [voters] that that person in Congress is not representing their district, they're only speaking for African Americans on the South Side of Chicago and Harlem. . . . Here is how we get reparations through. Initially, we have to provide economic security for all Americans. That is, since 90 percent of us are in the public school system, we should have a public education system of equal high quality for all Americans so we can explain to ignorant people what they don't know. We need to have a health care system in this country for all Americans so that those who do not have health care will not turn around and say, "That brother's getting health care, but I'm not getting health care," and using it as a political issue to create a wedge between us on that issue. We must provide everyone with health care. We must provide all four of those guys in Texas, that African American and those three white guys, and all Americans, with the constitutional right to have a job and not be sending our jobs overseas to foreign labor markets, undercutting organized and working men and women in this country. That is the preliminary step to making John Conyers's bill pass for all Americans. And then, white Democrats and white Republicans cannot use the argument that supporting something only for African Americans is not in the nation's interest. It is, when all Americans are economically secure. That's what I have to say about that. It's a tough issue, a tough issue.

Ogletree: One of the issues that we haven't touched upon at all . . . there are many more colors to the rainbow now. If you look at Texas or Florida or Louisiana, or California, or Arizona or New Mexico, you are seeing a whole new set of coalitions. And a whole new set of political points of view. What must we do in terms of the new paradigm to seriously and concretely create meaningful and thoughtful relationships with Latino-Americans, with Asian-Americans? Where have we failed and how do we go forward in thinking that everything is due to us, when now the populations are growing faster, the power is grow-

ing faster? How do we coalition-build as part of the new paradigm in the new millennium?

Guinier: I think that it's really important that we start to imagine
where we want to go and not just where we have been.
Obviously, we need to understand where we have been, but
we need to have a vision that other people want to follow us
to. So, for example, in Texas, after the Fifth Circuit outlawed
affirmative action at the University of Texas, a group of Black
and Latino professors, community activists, and legislators got
together to figure out: What should access to higher education in Texas look like? And they discovered that even though
affirmative action was a policy they had supported, that affirmative action was, in some ways, camouflaging the way in
which 150 privileged suburban and private schools had dominated access to the flagship schools in Texas. So you had
1,500 high schools in Texas and only 150 of them were sending most of their graduates to the University of Texas or Texas
A&M, the two flagship schools. So they looked and saw that
the real problem in Texas was the use of the SAT. The SAT
test was not predicting performance in college, but it was being used to keep out poor and working-class whites as well as
Black and Brown high school graduates. They then . . . got the
legislature to adopt a 10 percent plan so that anyone graduating in the top 10 percent of their high school class was automatically eligible for admission to the two flagship schools.
This was a plan that was supported initially by the Hispanic
and Black legislators, but they also got rural white legislators
to go along with it, because they showed them that the prior
plan [that] depended on the SAT was denying their con-
stituents access to this public good. Governor Bush signed the

legislation. He now takes credit for the legislation. And as a result of this new plan, more African Americans are at the University of Texas than were there under affirmative action. More Hispanics are at the University of Texas than were there under affirmative action. And those suburban and private high schools no longer dominate access to this school and, in fact, some rural counties in West Texas have sent graduates to this publicly funded school for the first time. But here's the P.S. Those students who have come in under the 10 percent plan, meaning they were in the top 10 percent of their graduating class, are doing better academically than all of the freshmen who had been admitted to the University of Texas prior to this Fifth Circuit decision. So what these Black and Hispanic legislators and activists did, by joining together, was to imagine a new vision of public education that was truly public and truly about education and not just about passing on privilege from one generation of privileged people to another. So to me, this is the new paradigm. Where Black and Brown people lead in a movement for justice, not just us.

Cole: It's not a question of race versus gender versus class. It is all and more. It is not electoral politics versus grassroots organizing. It is both. And, in fact, that it is not in coalition with others or only going it on our own, it is both. And to have the sophistication to choose. To me, there's always a very basic question: What is the job to be done? That will tell me what instrument to bring to do the job. Now, if I want to clean the house, do I use a dishwasher? Disastrous results. And so, if the issue requires an instrument of coalition of Black and Brown and Red and Yellow and progressive white people, let us bring that to it. But for those things which require us as a people to do for ourselves, let us do that too. I am convinced, for example, that there are bases on which we as Black women must organize, must take the leadership, and must bring justice for all women and all people. But there are other issues which we as Black women alone cannot address. Ask what is the job to be done and then bring the instrument. Finally, one point that has not been raised throughout the afternoon. I am really convinced that our ability as individuals should not be pitted against collective organizing. We need both. And each of us in this room is privileged. We wouldn't be here [otherwise]. Who are you helping to bring along? In Mary McLeod Bethune's words, "While we are in the process of lifting ourselves, we better make sure we're lifting somebody else too." And I am convinced that there's a responsibility for government, there's a responsibility for the corporate world to start understanding where their profits come from, there's a responsibility for our foundations and social service organizations, but I invite everyone here to do something as basic as mentor a young Black girl or boy.

Robinson: I wanted to take [an] opportunity to say a word in response to what Congressman Jackson said about reparations. I think it's important that we do not put the cart before the horse here. This thing is run somewhat like a trial. First you must establish culpability. And then we decide what the remedy is. I think America has, in the main, the largest problem with acceptance of responsibility. It is not the issue of money. This country spends un-Godly sums of money on things most Americans never even know about. It is not the money issue. It is the issue of denial. You know, it's like it never happened . . . we need to raise the dead who suffered and give them names. Because in remembering them, we can remember our own worth and what we're trying to do. We cannot let a nation tell us that it never happened. And so we have to force this acceptance. There's an anger now about that. It was a long time ago. I grew up in segregation. It was just yesterday. We're not talking just about 246 years from Jamestown on. We're talking about a century of de-jure segregation tacked on to the end of it. We're talking about perhaps the largest crime of all. The stripping of a people of their memory of who they were. And so, in the last analysis, we must come away from this with an understanding of what the value of this demand means. Whether we win or lose, what it means to us. To lose is one thing, to not have demanded what is your just due is the largest crime of all.

West: There's a relation between the literal dead and the living dead. Elijah Muhammad said, "I used to look in the South Side of Chicago and see the walking dead. These people need to learn how to die and white supremacy must die in order for them to live." That means that every Black person needs to get up every morning and squeeze the slave out of their minds, heart, and soul to be free. To be free. And the reason why we listen to our music is because in those moans and groans there's a connection between the struggle against the dead in the past and the dead in the present. And once we free our minds and hearts and souls, then we can tell the truth about ourselves and America and the world. And we can organize and mobilize and love each other enough to embrace one another even when we disagree and bring some power and pressure on the white supremacists of America.

Jones: I think that anything that will change in your life has to begin with how you think about yourself. There is no way for your life to change, there's no way for you to have the proper coalitions, there's no way for you to have the right kind of humility that goes with unity, there is no way for us to go forward unless we begin to think differently of ourselves. No one who oppresses you is going to give you the remedy for how you think about yourself. And there is no theology or religious entity that is truly representing God if it doesn't help us to change how we think about ourselves. The way we treat each other is a reflection of how we think about ourselves. And when we begin to love ourselves . . . we cannot just stay victims forever. We have to somehow find the strength that has sustained us all this time, to cause us to have the miracle of rebirth of how we think about ourselves, and we'll lift our heads up and we'll walk through this community, we will join hands with our brothers and sisters and we will lead men and women from the slave mentality into the freedom of the power of a free thinker.

Jackson Jr.: The opposite of big is small, the opposite of tall is short, the opposite of fat is skinny, and the opposite of high is low, the opposite of narrow is wide. I used to think that the opposite of love was hate, but I now know a little bit different now that I'm older and more mature. At least with the negative emotion called hate you at least care enough to have a negative emotion. But the opposite of love is indifference. Where we don't care at all. I used to think that the opposite of violence was nonviolence. But then I began to appreciate that we lived in a political, an economic, a social and educational and environmental context. And, therefore, the opposite of violence in this country is full employment. And that's why in the white community, where the economy is doing well, there's little crime. But in our community, where they have not invested and where it is not growing, we see violence. And that brings us to our central problem. That America has issued us a bad check. It has come back marked INSUFFICIENT FUNDS, and that she has defaulted on this obligation, insofar as her citizens of color are concerned. And that there will neither be rest nor tranquillity . . . until that obligation is met, until America honors these not so self-evident rights. . . . I have tried to argue today that those rights are the right to a public education of equal high quality, since that's where our children are, that those rights are the right to health care of high quality, that those rights are the right to a decent, safe, and affordable home, that those rights should come in the form of a job, and that those rights, those constitutional rights, should come in the form of a clean, safe, and sustainable environment. Since the only way to codify them in the law and ensure that our children and our children's children will always be the beneficiary of an America that is constantly repenting for the legacy—the institution of slavery as catapulted and expressed by both Democrats and Republicans for the last 140 years—codify them, not in a law, but in the Constitution. And if, in fact, that takes place . . . we will not only build a more perfect union for all Americans, we will build a more perfect world in every democracy throughout the world.

Giovanni: As a storyteller, I think it's so important that we tell . . . the stories that we know, that we tell the stories that we're living. I have a great love of the hip-hop generation because they're telling the story. I know a lot of people are upset, but I love 'em. Because somebody has to call a motherf—er a motherf—er, and they're doing that. That's what they're doing. . . . I think . . . all of us, we have to acknowledge what the kids bring to us, and we have, 'cause we want you all to acknowledge what we bring to you. . . . I think it's a really tremendous thing to be a Black American and I hope that we continue to draw on that strength.

Akbar: One of the key ideas that I've tried to develop in my writings and my work is the idea that the real empowerment of human beings is rooted in self-knowledge. That as we know who we are, we become automatically empowered with consciousness to transform our environment. So the process of empowerment, ultimately, is always a process of expanding the consciousness of who we are, what our makeup is, what our origins are, and what our destiny is. . . .

Bakewell: We have got to define ourselves. We have got to have vision for what tomorrow looks like for us in our community. And we've got to use all of this talent and all of this wealth of intellectual capacity, but we've got to couple that with activism in terms of doing something. We can't just leave here remembering what somebody said, we've got to use that as a diagram for what we're going to do. We've got to make sure that when we walk out in our communities, we're looking at job sites, and the people are not working who look like us. We're saying, "If we can't work, you can't work." We've got to call the police into accountability in our community and say we're not going to allow you to harm our children anymore. Because we're going to raise up in a major, major way and confront police brutality and demand police reform. We're going to be on all of the issues that we've talked about today, in a way that promotes activism, whether it be in education,

whether it be in all of the places that we know we need to create a quality of life for our children for tomorrow.

Cole: When I was growing up in Jacksonville, Florida, my
mother told me that a woman would be known by the company she keeps. And I just want to say how proud I am to be
in the company of these sisters and brothers. And to be in
your company. Who dares to say that we don't care, when you
are here? We got to educate, we got to legislate, and we got to
agitate. And any notion that activism—if I can give an amen
and an awomen, too—is no longer on our agenda, is to give
ourselves up eternally to the absence of freedom. . . . From
the West Coast [of Africa] the Ibo people say in a way that
captures, I think, education, action, spirituality, caring, "Not
to know is bad. Not to want to know is worse. Not to hope is
unthinkable. Not to care, and therefore to act, is unforgiv-
able."

Guinier: Leadership is not going to come from Washington. It is
not going to come from whoever is elected president in
November. Leadership is going to come from the people who
are seated here in this auditorium. Leadership is going to come
from the people who are out there all over the country. And so,
if we can act on this new vision of leadership that is not about
finding a charismatic or, as Cornel said or as Randall said, a
messianic leader, leadership is about understanding that we
need to act together, because alone we cannot do the things
that we can do together. And that is an asset that Black people
have that we should be proud of, that we understand the importance of solidarity, we understand the importance of collective
action, we understand the importance of thinking systemically,
we understand the importance of taking when it is needed. And

I think the unfortunate thing about the whole last twenty-five years is that we have been made . . . to think that somehow we can hand over the baton to other people who will act on our behalf. No one is going to act for us, although they may act with us, if we show them the way.

Vanzant: I am a Yoruba priestess, which means by definition that I am a cultural custodian. It is my job in the embodiment of the flesh form as a female to keep alive the culture and the energy and the traditions of my ancestors. However, that cultural knowledge must evolve and become prevalent in and practiced in the day in which we are now. So as a cultural custodian, as a keeper of the traditions of the Yoruba people, I believe that in the new paradigm, one of the things that we have to do is to eliminate againstness. You don't have to be against anything—just be clear about what you're for. If we could just be clear about what we are for, what we are standing for, what we are living for, what we are bringing forth—our brother Randall said earlier, to bring forth the dead and give it a name. So as you bring forth your grandmother, what are you standing for on behalf of her life so that she will look good in the new millennium? . . . As a Yoruba priestess, I know the power of the word. Because it was part of our culture as African people to speak the word with dominion, power, and authority. And know that we could call a thing that is not, as if it is and it will be. So as we stand today, in this place, we have to no longer call ourselves in trouble, but call ourselves great. Call forth your greatness, stand in your bigness, declare your freedom, and take the actions with your grandmother bringing up the rear that'll get you to where you say you're going. Declare it right now. Finally, I think that as a Yoruba priestess . . .

[you've] got to have a good head. Because no man can be blessed without the spirit of his own head. People can't even be good to you, unless you're willing to receive the goodness that they bring. So it's about cleaning up our own heads and our own thoughts. And the way that we can do that is to step out of the intellect into the spirit. Because that's where your grandmother is. That's where your great-grandfather is. That's where Ptah is. That's where Imhotep is. That's where Het Heru is. That's where Harriet [Tubman] is. That's where the Christ is. It ain't up here, it's in there. So if we can just step down, from our opinions, our likes and dislikes, from being pissed off with people, from what we think about people, from our gossiping about people. If we could just step down from that and move faithfully to the core of our being, your ancestors will download the information that you need. They will download it into your being. And then all you have to do is push F7 and talk. Stand up in your bigness. Be clear about what you're for. Call a thing that is not, as if it is and it will be yours.

Ogletree: What I'm hearing is a whole new attitude, and I think for the first time in my life that we have touched our ancestral heritage in the hundreds of thousands and millions of Africans who never made it here, and those who died here know today we do care about the past and we are creating new paradigms for African Americans to go into the new millennium. . . . We didn't come here to talk about ourselves, and what we did was to learn from you. We know your frustrations, your pain, your anger, your anxiety. It's all justified. But . . . we can't just complain about it. We've got to do something about it. We've got to get involved. We can't be talking about each other, who's with who. We've got to get activated. . . . No

one [here today] said, "I made it on my own." No one said,
"I'm gifted." No one said, "I'm here because I'm great." We
stand on the shoulders of people who've sacrificed. That's why
we're here today. . . . Today, we outlined an agenda, we talked
about the future. We have to come back and . . . work on education, work on employment, work on health care, work on
voter involvement. What we have to do is to say it's not just
enough to . . . talk about the problems. . . . Let's become the
solution-makers in our community.

ALSO BY TAVIS SMILEY

"Tavis Smiley writes like he talks. . . . Clear, passionate, and
to the point."   —*Detroit Free Press*

DOING WHAT'S RIGHT

*How to Fight for What You
Believe—and Make a Difference*

In an impassioned call to arms, Tavis Smiley sets forth the
tools we can use to stand up for what we believe and help
improve our communities, our lives, and our world.

Smiley isn't alone in pointing out that our neighborhoods
are unsafe, our communities are unraveling, and our most
basic values —civility, a sense of justice, responsibility, and
integrity—are under attack. But we don't have to put up
with a world gone awry. We don't need to play the blame
game. We are neither helpless nor are we victims.

In *Doing What's Right*, Smiley shows how each one of us
can combat complacency and fight for the causes in which
we believe. By choosing the battles that matter most to us
and organizing a plan to bring about the changes we feel
are necessary, we can transform the world around us. For
everyone who genuinely wants to be a voice for change,
Doing What's Right is a must-read.

Self Help/African American Studies/0-385-49931-0

Order the historic "Black Think Tank" symposium now!

Advocacy in the New Millennium: New Paradigms for Progress, live recording held at the University of Southern California on August 12, 2000.

Quantity

Advocacy Series Vol. 2
Advocacy in the New Millennium: New Paradigms for Progress
VHS 4 hrs., Panels 1 & 2
$_____$40 ($6.50 S&H)

Advocacy Series Vol. 2
Advocacy in the New Millennium: New Paradigms for Progress
Audiocassettes
$_____Panel 1 180 min. $15 ($4.50 S&H)
$_____Panel 2 180 min. $15 ($4.50 S&H)

$_____**Subtotal**
$_____Shipping & Handling (add $2 S&H for each add'l quantity)
$_____California residents add 8.25% sales tax
$_____**Total Enclosed or Authorized**

(Please print all information requested)

Name _____

Billing Address_____

Ship to (if different)_____

City/State/Zip_____

Phone_____ Fax_____

Method of payment

Visa   MC   Amex   Check enclosed

Account#

Expiration date

Signature _____

Make checks payable/mail to: The Smiley Group, Inc., 3870 Crenshaw Blvd., pmb 391, Los Angeles, CA 90008 or fax your credit card order to (323) 290-3940. Please allow 3 to 4 weeks for delivery.

To place your order online, go to: *http//www.tavistalks.com*